"Joe Emison is the apostle of leverage in technical managed services for scale and speed while putting d tribute maximum business value. Leaders bold enoug brilliant book will reap outsized rewards."

— *Forrest Brazeal, Head of Developer Media at Google Cloud*

"Joe's been telling the world for years that modern software architecture isn't just about getting rid of your servers, but deleting most of your server code. It's a message that bucks conventional wisdom, and the "best practices" of the kubernetes-industrial complex. But here's the weird thing—he might just be right."

— *Mike Roberts, Partner and Co-founder, Symphonia*

"This book backs up theory with the real-world practices that Joe has been successfully implementing as a business strategy for years. It is a handbook for modern development teams that want to deliver value faster, more securely, and with less technical debt."

— *Jeremy Daly, CEO at Ampt and AWS Serverless Hero*

"*Serverless as a Game Changer* is an indispensable book, guiding startups and enterprises to better business outcomes. With its technical expertise, it unveils the power of Serverless applications, focusing on organizational needs and risk mitigation. If you aim to embrace cutting-edge tech and build Serverless solutions, this is a must-read."

$PrintCode

— *Farrah Campbell, Head of Modern Compute Community, AWS*

"A must-read for executives and technologists who want to go faster and capture more business value for less. Serverless will change the way you build businesses with technology, and this book will show you how."

— *Yan Cui, AWS Serverless Hero*

Serverless as a Game Changer

  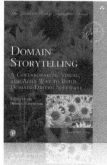 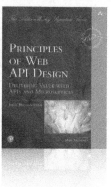

Serverless as a Game Changer

How to Get the Most Out of the Cloud

Joseph Emison

For information about buying this title in bulk quantities, or for special sales opportunities (which may include electronic versions; custom cover designs; and content particular to your business, training goals, marketing focus, or branding interests), please contact our corporate sales department at corpsales@pearsoned.com or (800) 382-3419.

For government sales inquiries, please contact governmentsales@pearsoned.com.

For questions about sales outside the U.S., please contact intlcs@pearson.com.

Visit us on the Web: informit.com/aw

Library of Congress Control Number: 2023944699

Copyright © 2024 Pearson Education, Inc.

Hoboken, New Jersey

Cover image: Irina Soboleva S / Shutterstock

ISBN-13: 978-0-13-739262-9
ISBN-10: 0-13-739262-1

$PrintCode

Pearson's Commitment to Diversity, Equity, and Inclusion

Pearson is dedicated to creating bias-free content that reflects the diversity of all learners. We embrace the many dimensions of diversity, including but not limited to race, ethnicity, gender, socioeconomic status, ability, age, sexual orientation, and religious or political beliefs.

Education is a powerful force for equity and change in our world. It has the potential to deliver opportunities that improve lives and enable economic mobility. As we work with authors to create content for every product and service, we acknowledge our responsibility to demonstrate inclusivity and incorporate diverse scholarship so that everyone can achieve their potential through learning. As the world's leading learning company, we have a duty to help drive change and live up to our purpose to help more people create a better life for themselves and to create a better world.

Our ambition is to purposefully contribute to a world where

- Everyone has an equitable and lifelong opportunity to succeed through learning
- Our educational products and services are inclusive and represent the rich diversity of learners
- Our educational content accurately reflects the histories and experiences of the learners we serve
- Our educational content prompts deeper discussions with learners and motivates them to expand their own learning (and worldview)

While we work hard to present unbiased content, we want to hear from you about any concerns or needs with this Pearson product so that we can investigate and address them.

Please contact us with concerns about any potential bias at https://www.pearson.com/report-bias.html.

Contents

Foreword

When I was introduced to Joe Emison (nearly three years ago at the time of writing this foreword) I was very impressed by his knowledge of serverless. It's not that Joe—a serial entrepreneur CTO—knows more about the entire topic than other cloud experts, although he probably does in a lot of cases. What impressed me the most is his understanding of how to use cloud serverless and managed services to truly improve the software's production behaviors and dependability, all while saving a lot of money as a result. And when I say, "saving a lot of money," I mean a staggering amount. I've heard of startups going under due to unexpected cloud costs, such as the surprise invoice for US $100,000+ for one month. At the time that I met Joe, his startup, Branch, was spending a whopping US $800 per month on everything cloud and serverless. Try to beat that. Since then, he's kept costs way down and company value way up by delivering good software with customer value that always stays running. The bottom line is that Joe is solving business problems first by using technology intelligently. He's been successful to the extent that his company became a unicorn in 2022, just four years after starting up. Without a doubt, Joe knows business and he knows the business of software. And his track record started long before Branch. I explain more below about Joe's stellar, success-rendering approaches to cloud-native systems.

My Signature Series is designed and curated to guide readers toward advances in software development maturity and greater success with business-centric practices. The series emphasizes organic refinement with a variety of approaches—reactive, object, as well as functional architecture and programming; domain modeling; right-sized services; patterns; and APIs—and covers best uses of the associated underlying technologies.

From here I am focusing now on only two words: organic refinement.

The first word, *organic*, stood out to me recently when a friend and colleague used it to describe software architecture. I have heard and used the word *organic* in connection with software development, but I didn't think about that word as carefully as I did then when I personally consumed the two used together: *organic architecture*.

Think about the word *organic*, and even the word *organism*. For the most part these are used when referring to living things, but they are also used to describe inanimate things that feature some characteristics that resemble life forms. *Organic* originates in Greek. Its etymology is with reference to a functioning organ of the body. If you read the etymology of *organ*, it has a broader use, and in fact organic followed suit: body organs; to implement; describes a tool for making or doing; a musical instrument.

We can readily think of numerous organic objects—living organisms—from the very large to the microscopic single-celled life forms. With the second use of organism, though, examples may not as readily pop into our mind. One example is an organization, which includes the prefix of both *organic* and *organism*. In this use of *organism*, I'm describing something that is structured with bidirectional dependencies. An organization is an organism because it has organized parts. This kind of organism cannot survive without the parts, and the parts cannot survive without the organism.

Taking that perspective, we can continue applying this thinking to nonliving things because they exhibit characteristics of living organisms. Consider the atom. Every single atom is a system unto itself, and all living things are composed of atoms. Yet, atoms are inorganic and do not reproduce. Even so, it's not difficult to think of atoms as living things in the sense that they are endlessly moving, functioning. Atoms even bond with other atoms. When this occurs, each atom is not only a single system unto itself but becomes a subsystem along with other atoms as subsystems, with their combined behaviors yielding a greater whole system.

So then, all kinds of concepts regarding software are quite organic in that nonliving things are still "characterized" by aspects of living organisms. When we discuss software model concepts using concrete scenarios, or draw an architecture diagram, or write a unit test and its corresponding domain model unit, software starts to come alive. It isn't static, because we continue to discuss how to make it better, subjecting it to refinement, where one scenario leads to another, and that has an impact on the architecture and the domain model. As we continue to iterate, the increasing value in refinements leads to incremental growth of the organism. As time progresses so does the software. We wrangle with and tackle complexity through useful abstractions, and the software grows and changes shapes, all with the explicit purpose of making work better for real living organisms at global scales.

Sadly, software organics tend to grow poorly more often than they grow well. Even if they start out life in good health they tend to get diseases, become deformed, grow unnatural appendages, atrophy, and deteriorate. Worse still is that these symptoms are caused by efforts to refine the software that go wrong instead of making things better. The worst part is that with every failed refinement, everything that goes wrong with these complexly ill bodies doesn't cause their death. Oh, if they could just die! Instead, we have to kill them, and killing them requires nerves, skills, and the intestinal fortitude of a dragon slayer. No, not one, but dozens of vigorous dragon slayers. Actually, make that dozens of dragon slayers who have really big brains.

That's where this series comes into play. I am curating a series designed to help you mature and reach greater success with a variety of approaches—reactive, object, and functional architecture and programming; domain modeling; right-sized services; patterns; and APIs. And along with that, the series covers best uses of the associated underlying technologies. It's not accomplished at one fell swoop. It requires organic refinement with purpose and skill. I and the other authors are here to help. To that end, we've delivered our very best to achieve our goal.

Considering my goals, I couldn't pass up the opportunity to include Joe's book in my Signature Series. "It's not my uptime" is Joe's fundamental thinking on using serverless. It's not a cliché. It's smart computing.

I was impressed that Joe uses multiple cloud providers for what they do best. That might sound obvious, but I don't mean just AWS, Google Cloud, and Azure. Would most CTOs consider using Netlify, and later switching to Vercel with little rework, to serve Web content and application functionality? I doubt it, and in my experience, no they wouldn't. Yet, Joe has proven how powerful, practical, and cost effective that is. How many chief architects would insist on using a fully managed cloud search service rather than tweaking, contributing to, and self-managing ElasticSearch? In my experience, not many. Every single time that Joe could use a cloud-managed service rather than building a service or use a self-managed software product, he chooses managed services. He weaved it into company culture. What CTO would have the patience to hire and train JavaScript frontend developers to build serverless applications? Joe does, and his people learn quickly. Which architect or developer would choose to build a small-footprint monolith that's deployed as a set of serverless functions? Joe has delivered around 12 of those so far, rather than hundreds or thousands of tiny functions. That's not all. I've only scratched the surface. Joe is an example in business computing and his book is a master class on *Serverless as a Game Changer*. So read on and persuade others in technology leadership roles to do the same.

—Vaughn Vernon, series editor

Register your copy of *Serverless as a Game Changer* on the InformIT site for convenient access to updates and/or corrections as they become available. To start the registration process, go to informit.com/register and log in or create an account. Enter the product ISBN (9780137392629) and click Submit. Look on the Registered Products tab for an Access Bonus Content link next to this product, and follow that link to access any available bonus materials. If you would like to be notified of exclusive offers on new editions and updates, please check the box to receive email from us.

Acknowledgments

I would like to thank my wife, Abbie, and children, Seamus, Grace, and Amelia, who have been a consistent source of support. It wouldn't be possible or enjoyable to write a book without you.

Special thanks to Vaughn Vernon, whose invitation to put my thoughts on how to build Serverlessly several years ago pushed me into action.

Holly Tachovsky and Steve Lekas, thank you both for being amazing co-founders who encouraged me to build software and run tech organizations in the way that I saw would be best, as opposed to judging me by any past/other standards you had encountered.

Thank you to all the reviewers of early drafts of this book: Ben Kehoe and Mike Roberts, thank you for your subject-matter expertise and encouragement to make the book stronger and more applicable to specific leaders and executives. Joel Goldberg, thank you for your stakeholder expertise and excellent questions about how to apply the advice you read. And Geraldine Powell (my mother!), thank you for your help in making the book much clearer for everyone.

I would like to thank everyone at Pearson, and especially Haze Humbert, for your kindness and support along the way.

And finally, I would like to thank my parents, who supported me (financially and emotionally) to pursue software development at an early age with Turbo Pascal 5.0 in 1994, and to my uncle, Jon Masters, who bought me *Turbo Pascal by Example* by Greg Perry, which brought me over that huge initial hurdle every software developer must overcome.

About the Author

Joe Emison is the co-founder and CTO of Branch, a personal lines insurance company. Before Branch, Joe built five other companies as a technical co-founder, across many industries, including consumer electronics, local government, big data analysis, and commercial real estate. Joe graduated with degrees in English and Mathematics from Williams College and has a law degree from Yale Law School.

Figure Credits

Chapter 1

Introduction

The gap between the best software development teams and average software development teams is enormous. The best teams deliver delightful, scalable, stable software to users quickly and regularly. Average teams deliver acceptable software that works most of the time, with months or even years between significant improvements. Many teams even struggle to deliver anything but small, iterative changes, with even those taking surprising amounts of time. Software development and cloud services and tools make developing and deploying software increasingly cheaper, faster, and better—but very few organizations take advantage of these innovations. This book lays out the principles, strategies, and tactics that can propel your organization or teams to world-class output by harnessing a Serverless mindset.

Historically, to deliver web-scale applications with wonderful customer experience, organizations have had to hire expensive, superior talent in many disciplines: networking, infrastructure, systems administration, software architecture, back-end software development, API design, and front-end application design. The demand for these talented employees has always exceeded the number of them, and most companies have simply been unable to acquire talent that would enable them to build products such as a Google or Netflix.

That world has changed, and building web-scale, world-class applications is now possible without needing to hire any "ninja" or "rockstar" developers. Serverless applications leverage the immense talent within cloud providers and managed services to solve the hard problems of building and scaling complex infrastructure and software systems. The average developer today is more capable of delivering the next Gmail or TikTok than the most talented, expensive team of developers 10 years ago. Organizations with solid, attainable development teams can leapfrog their competitors by leveraging a Serverless approach and building applications differently, to deliver like the top-notch software teams in the world.

Perhaps most important, building Serverlessly enables organizations to concentrate on what makes them unique and to focus investments on differentiated projects. Organizations can stop spending enormous amounts of budget on projects that no one except the software development team can even understand. Customers do not care that an organization is running a world-class Kubernetes cluster with hundreds of thousands of lines of customization; customers want their experience to be world class. Just as cloud adoption over the past 15 years has enabled every organization to build web-scale applications, Serverless enables every organization to deliver software as efficiently and effectively as the best software teams in the world.

The winners will be the organizations that change their games by recognizing how to build Serverlessly first. These companies will be able to accelerate the delivery of new products, services, and features for their customers because they will not be focusing on the commodity plumbing that underpins world-class software. They will leverage managed services with the best software developers in the world for services that are non-differentiating for their business, to allow them to focus more on building highly specific interfaces and logic for their customers. Ultimately, they will outpace, outmaneuver, and create unmatchable cost structures over any competitors that are slow to adapt to this new way of working.

How Many Employees Does It Take to Make and Run a Scalable Social Network?

In the recent history of software development, one of the hardest services to build and launch has been a scalable social network. Social networks need to be fast, always be online, and scale to ever-increasing traffic as they become more successful. One of the first popular social networks, Friendster, famously lost its lead because of its inability to scale[1] and was subsequently eclipsed by Myspace and Facebook, both of which had hundreds of employees supporting their builds.

Fast-forward to 2014, and a curiously simple social network called Yo launched. Members could sign up quickly, choose people or organizations to follow, and send only one message: "Yo!" In the first few days after its public launch on both iOS and Android, Yo scaled successfully to more than a million users; more than 100 million "Yo!" messages were delivered before it shut down in 2016.[2]

Yo was built by one developer (initially in about 8 hours) and never needed systems administrators, operations teams, or even full-time developers for its initial ramp existence.[3] Somewhat ironically, all the Yo code was being run and scaled by Facebook, which had acquired one of the first Backend as a Service companies,

How Many Employees Does It Take to Make and Run a Scalable
Social Network?

3

Parse. Yo leveraged Facebook's engineering and operational expertise in its Parse division, paying only $100 a month to handle 40 requests per second with 1 million unique push-notification recipients.[4, 5]

You can see this same leverage of managed services by Instagram, which had 13 employees at the time Facebook acquired it for $1 billion.[6] Of the 13, only 3 were full-time software developers; Instagram had no dedicated systems administrators or operations staff.

A relatively short time after Friendster was crushed by its inability to handle web traffic with hundreds of employees, two startups with only a handful of software developers conquered the same challenges with ease (see Figure 1.1).[7, 8] They did so by outsourcing much of the required expertise to newly created managed-service providers, who handled the "running and scaling infrastructure" expertise.[9]

An easy answer to the question posed by the title of this section, then, is that the number of employees needed to make and run a scalable social network approaches zero over time (absent moderation). Many components that both Instagram and Yo had to build are now much easier to handle, around a decade later. Many organizations spend so much time and effort building infrastructure, systems, and code that they could rent at a fraction of the price, with no dedicated personnel and with substantially better performance and uptime. It is amazing that organizations continue to compete on the playing field against Amazon, Google, or Microsoft when they could simply incorporate Amazon or Google's great players into their own teams by going Serverless.

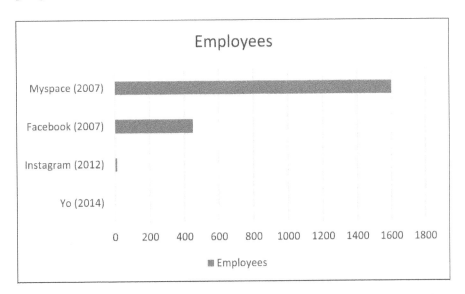

Figure 1.1 *Number of Employees Needed to Make and Run a Scalable Social Network over Time*

Leveraging Technology as It Improves

Software Development Has Been Improving Constantly...

Technology moves quickly. Moore's Law, that the number of transistors that can fit on a chip doubles every two years, has an equivalent in the software development world: The best way to build a piece of software from scratch gets a little bit easier every year. Often these small incremental changes are missed.

Everyone sees and recognizes that big tectonic shifts such as the public cloud have changed the game. Organizations that were slow to adapt have fallen behind, whereas others that recognized this shift and adapted have been able to win in the marketplace. But these big shifts are only part of the story. Hundreds of new services launched every year improve software development and provide meaningful benefits to organizations willing to incorporate them into their software.

Tasks that were extremely challenging 10 years ago, such as reliably resizing images, performing a fuzzy text search with tens of gigabytes of data, or handling hundreds of millions of monthly visitors from around the globe in milliseconds, are now often as simple to achieve as plugging a lamp into a wall. This is because technological improvements are not built in isolation; they are built on top of other technological innovations.

Thus, if one innovation per year can double output, then after 10 years, output could be increased by $2^{10} = 1,024$ times, not $2 \times 10 = 20$ times. This rate of innovation far exceeds what any one organization can build, so the benefit of learning how to harness it for an organization far exceeds the value of being the most innovative organization, building the maximum that the organization can build.

...But Isn't Being Adopted Effectively

If innovation in technology—specifically, in how to build software more efficiently and effectively—is happening and making development so much easier, why are these changes not being widely adopted?

Sadly, there is no continuing education in information technology. Most managers, architects, and senior staff in IT departments also have no set expectations that they should be regularly changing how they do their job, as new technology comes out. It is torture for someone to learn how to do something at the start of their career and then, after several successful years, throw out that knowledge and start again. The benefits of change must be intuitively obvious because so much personal and organizational inertia surrounds the industry. Even then, real change often requires significant changes in culture, mindset, architecture, coding practices, and technology leadership.

Additionally, even if teams identify significant changes they want to make, they still are called upon to deliver new features and functionality within their existing technology stacks. An organization that identifies changes it wants to make in how it builds and runs software must have buy-in and coordination at all levels in order to make significant changes.

The most successful people do two jobs: the job they were hired to do and the job of figuring out how to do that primary job better. This is a required mentality for everyone working on, in, and around the best software development teams. It is especially difficult in software development because of the rapid rate of change. Constantly thinking about how to do a job better, even if it requires learning brand new skills and doing jobs differently, is the only way to take full advantage of technology—and is the right way to approach reading this book.

This Book Is For...

Executives in Business and Technology

I have written this book for both business-minded technologists and technology-minded businesspeople. Increasingly, if you are a businessperson, you must be technology minded because, as is often quoted, "software is eating the world."[10] More companies are increasingly becoming software companies. Whether you are a business-minded technologist or a technology-minded businessperson, this book teaches you how to build and deploy software better, faster, cheaper, and more effectively than most companies in the world.

If you are a senior business leader, this book helps you bring technological change into your organization by showing you how a Serverless approach drives better business outcomes. If you are a technical team lead, this book helps you think like an executive leader and focus more on delivering value than optimizing for tech, to set you apart from your peers. You will increase your focus on what matters to your organization, release new features and functionality more quickly, and spend less money, time, and effort doing it. You will learn how to do all this while also learning how to mitigate the risks that are inherent when you rely on third parties to be successful.

Enterprises

I have run technology at companies of all sizes, and Serverless is just as beneficial for enterprises as brand-new startups. Enterprises will likely get the most benefit of adopting a Serverless mindset over their similarly sized competitors than startups because most enterprises suffer from more technical debt and an internal discontent with software development velocity. The journey within an enterprise to build fully Serverless applications is a long one that involves as much cultural as technical transformation. Part III of this book, "Getting to Serverless," focuses on the key steps to drive Serverless adoption within an enterprise.

Startups and Smaller Businesses

Serverless is a game changer for startups and smaller businesses because it enables them to run lean budgets and use small numbers of developers to deliver software and services that look like they come from teams orders of magnitude larger. Branch, which I founded (and which is discussed in more detail in Part II, "Real-World Serverless"), has operated with approximately 1/30th (that is, around 97% less) the developer payroll of an insurance startup that launched fewer products in fewer states than Branch. Part III is mainly targeted at larger and more established organizations, but it is also useful for startups because the cultural and technical transitions are much the same.

This Book Is Not About...

Service-Oriented Architectures

Serverless applications generally have service-oriented architectures (SOAs), with some custom code calling managed services and other custom code acting as a service (as opposed to using a lot of repeated code in different, similar features).[11] Using unnecessarily repeated code or repeated bespoke functionality within Serverless applications is difficult because leveraging managed services is native and simple within Serverless architectures.

However, this book does not spend significant time talking about SOAs in the context of building Serverless applications. Much of the discussion surrounding SOAs is predicated on older, non-Serverless methods of building software. Once an organization adopts a Serverless mindset, developers are highly unlikely to stray from SOA patterns because of how natural the patterns are in Serverless.

Monoliths and Microservices

The monolith vs. microservice debate has raged for more than a decade. That age is increasingly apparent when viewed in light of Serverless development. Serverless architectures tend to muddy the definitional waters between the two strategies; many Serverless applications, including those at Branch, have characteristics of both.

For example, one factor that drove a lot of initial microservice development was concern about the uptime and scalability of databases. Netflix famously implemented microservices to increase the resilience of other systems, giving stateful microservices their own databases to prevent other database failures from impacting their uptime.[12] However, many Serverless applications use managed, resilient, global databases such as AWS DynamoDB that have incredible historical uptime and low latency. When using DynamoDB, the traditional microservice motivations for separation of concerns around the datastore no longer exist.

Another operational motivation for separation of concerns within microservices has been preventing cascading failures due to traffic overload on a particular service. However, if service code is running on a service such as AWS Lambda, Google Cloud Functions, or Azure Functions, those cloud providers have proven that they can prevent any kind of cascading failure because of the capacity and architecture they have built for running code.

Nevertheless, Serverless applications often feel more like microservice applications because of how they use services and how they tend to separate business concerns. In my experience, most Serverless applications are too broken up into separate functions (more on this in Chapter 3, "Serverless Architectures"). Branch's architecture at the time of publication consists of around 100 Lambda functions and 5 React applications, but all in a monorepo designed to be deployed monolithically. Definitionally, that's not a monolith or a microservices architecture, and I don't think the distinction is helpful when building Serverlessly.

No-Code/Low-Code Platforms

This book is built on the assumption that the organization has software developers who will use software development languages, frameworks, and environments. My experiences with no-code and low-code platforms have led me to believe that the only ones that really work are those that use standard languages and function as a higher-level framework that can be "ejected" (for example, Expo for React Native, or AWS Amplify for web applications)[13] so that the application can continue development in a more traditional development and/or hosting environment.

I believe that no- and low-code platforms have their place. We used one to build our initial interactive demo for Branch, which was a much faster and easier route than building it in code (and also less likely to lead us to technical debt). But ultimately, there is no comparison between what is possible with no- and low-code platforms versus fully fledged languages and frameworks. Building a customer-facing, business-critical application in a no- or low-code platform is risky because of how inherently limited the platforms are. Therefore, this book does not address any tools or services that I consider no- or low-code (that is, proprietary language and/or IDE combined with proprietary hosting and no ability to eject).

Structure of the Book

The first part of this book explains the Serverless mindset. The Serverless mindset is a way of developing, deploying, and running software in which an organization retains the responsibility for building differentiated experiences for its customers and uses managed services for everything else. The key to the Serverless mindset is separating assets versus liabilities and differentiated versus undifferentiated capabilities. The book walks through several detailed technical examples of Serverless architectures. Many technologists take a narrow view of Serverless; these examples help explain the broader picture and value that Serverless delivers. The last chapter in Part I, "The Serverless Mindset," addresses common objections to Serverless architectures and features several real-world case studies of Serverless in practice.

Part II compares Branch, the insurance company that I started in 2018, with the fictional Insureco, a representative enterprise insurance company. The goal of this part of the book is to give specific details on exactly how Branch handles all the intricacies of being a regulated, for-profit financial services company while being Serverless. This part also illustrates the massive benefits delivered over what might be considered a "best practices" enterprise today.

Part III tackles this question: "Okay, I buy all of this, but how can we get to Serverless from where we are now?" It considers the best metrics to use to align everyone across the business on how to measure success. It explains why the only viable method for making changes to existing systems is iterative replacement. Finally, it talks about continuing education and job retraining, which are critical parts of outsourcing functions that you no longer should have in-house.

Part III concludes with Chapter 11, "Your Serverless Journey," which brings together everything that was previously discussed. It lays out a high-level set of observations on how generally to think about building serverless applications, as well as a tactical outline for how you can approach building serverless applications.

Finally, Part IV, "Appendixes," and the companion website to this book feature a comprehensive listing of managed services, organized by category. Most people building software have no idea how much software developer time can be saved by leveraging managed services. Managed services can handle many functions of applications, from the core of an application, to authentication, search, image manipulation, customer communication, and even software development functions such as code review and testing. The directory provided herein gives examples and details that will help technologists and business leaders alike understand which services they can leverage today.

References

[1] Hoff, Todd. "Friendster Lost Lead Because of a Failure to Scale." http://high-scalability.com/blog/2007/11/13/friendster-lost-lead-because-of-a-failure-to-scale.html

[2] "MobileBeat 2014: How Did a Stupidly Simple App Get Such Stupidly Huge Growth?" (2014). www.youtube.com/watch?v=ZA-Hnd1j_II

[3] Shontell, Alyson. "The Inside Story of Yo: How a 'Stupid' App Attracted Millions of Dollars and Rocketed to the Top of the App Store." (June 21, 2014) www.businessinsider.com/the-inside-story-of-yo-there-isnt-actually-1-million-in-the-bank-2014-6

[4] Parse Plans and Pricing. (2014) http://web.archive.org/web/20140714210913/https://parse.com/plans

[5] Amazon Web Services Case Study: Yo. https://aws.amazon.com/solutions/case-studies/yo/

[6] "Instagram Is Celebrating Its 10th Birthday. A Decade After Launch, Here Is Where Its Original 13 Employees Have Ended Up." www.businessinsider.com/instagram-first-13-employees-full-list-2020-4

[7] Facebook Number of Employees. https://statinvestor.com/data/22188/facebook-number-of-employees/

[8] Yo (app). https://en.wikipedia.org/wiki/Yo_(app)

[9] Cutler, Kim-Mai, and Josh Constine. "Facebook Buys Parse to Offer Mobile Development Tools as Its First Paid B2B Service." (2003) https://techcrunch.com/2013/04/25/facebook-parse/

[10] Andreesen, Marc. "Software Is Eating the World." (2011) www.wsj.com/articles/SB10001424053111903480904576512250915629460

[11] Amazon: Service-Oriented Architectures. https://aws.amazon.com/what-is/service-oriented-architecture/

[12] "A Design Analysis of Cloud-based Microservices at Netflix." https://medium.com/swlh/a-design-analysis-of-cloud-based-microservices-architecture-at-netflix-98836b2da45f

[13] "Being Free from 'expo' in React Native Apps." https://medium.com/reactbrasil/being-free-from-expo-in-react-native-apps-310034a3729

Chapter 2

The Real Cost of Software Development

The critical missing element in most discussions about how best to build software is a common understanding of the real costs of software development. Internalizing the complete set of costs often helps organizations realize that purchasing software is usually significantly less expensive than building it. Usually, the most cost-effective choice is to leverage existing services, integrated with a small amount of custom-built code. This chapter enumerates the many different costs that organizations face, depending on how they choose to develop software. It also points out which elements of software development drive value to organizations and which are simply cost centers. Finally, the chapter explains how to apply this comprehensive view of cost and value to make better software development choices within the organization.

Types of Costs

Cost accounting is a practice that helps leaders make decisions by identifying all different types of costs.[1] This section lists and explains different types of costs. Why do you care about all these different costs? Understanding costs helps determine which of several options might be the right one. Each type of cost is relevant to building and running software, and many elements of these costs are often overlooked.

For example, imagine that an organization is evaluating two options: Option A does not cost anything up front, but it requires hiring several new employees and will take a year to deploy. Option B costs a significant amount up front but does not require any hiring and takes two weeks to deploy. Cost accounting helps leaders compare these options on a (roughly) apples-to-apples basis. The simplest way to use cost accounting in decision-making is to walk through the different types of costs, assign each one a present-value amount, and then compare those across alternatives (see Figure 2.1).

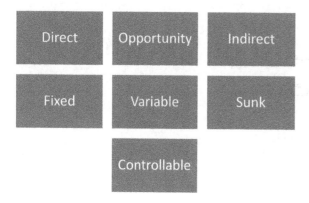

Figure 2.1 *Cost Accounting Categories in Software Development*

Direct Costs

Direct costs are the most obvious costs in software: They are the specific amounts of money spent directly on building and running the software. This includes software and library licensing and also the labor spent planning, developing, deploying, testing, and operating the software. Direct costs primarily are underestimated in software projects because there tends to be an assumption that the project will involve a large initial build of up to 18 months and that the number of people working on the project then will decrease. In reality, most software projects only ever have increasing amounts of labor allocated to them over their lifetimes, at least until they are put into maintenance mode or sunset.[2]

This miscalculation happens for many reasons. The primary reason is that software tends to need constant iteration, both because initial specifications are rarely completely correct and because users demand more features with each release. Not only do these challenges make it difficult to build successfully over time, but they also sometimes lead to projects never releasing a viable first version. Potential custom-built software solutions almost always are substantially more expensive than the purchase of Software-as-a-Service (SaaS) products with overlapping functionality. This is because the SaaS product's development is split across many customers, and software margins are not high enough to eclipse the cost difference. In addition, software developers and software product owners systematically underestimate the effort required to build a software product that they have used (or seen in demos), often because they don't understand that certain functionality will be built only after they have put some of the functionality into production.

Another reason for direct cost underestimation is that building software is fun. Software developers enjoy building software. Organizational leaders enjoy designing and being involved in software development projects, at least at the beginning. The people involved in pitching a software development project therefore often have rosier assumptions about their cost calculations than is warranted.

Table 2.1 lays out a short list of expensive failed (meaning never completed or launched) software projects as a good set of examples of direct cost miscalculation.[3]

Underestimating required direct costs for internal labor over time tends to swing decision makers away from buying services, software, or libraries as part of their software projects on an erroneous cost analysis basis (part of the Not Invented Here [NIH] syndrome). The best way for an organization to avoid NIH is for executives to understand that direct cost estimation about internal resources is often underestimated in a way that the direct cost estimation about external, third-party resources is not. People internally are generally far too optimistic about what they will be able to accomplish in a given period of time. Before embarking on an internal project of many months or years, it is at least worth getting an external opinion on how long that work is likely to take. One good way to get an external estimate of building internal software is to find another company that has built similar software and determine how long that process took.

Table 2.1 *Expensive Failed Software Projects*

Software System	Primary Problem	Estimated Cost (at End)
TAURUS trading platform (1980s–1993)	Scope creep	$102 million
Regional Information Systems Plan (1984–1990)	Scope creep	$85 million
Bolit, Swedish Patent and Registration Office System (1997–2000)	Too complicated	$35 million
Centre for Study of Insurance Operations Portal (1999–2006)	Low user adoption	$12 million
Expeditionary Combat Support System (2005–2012)	Massively underscoped	$1.1 billion
Da:Polsag Policy Case Management (2007–2012)	Did not function	$70 million
UK e-Borders (2007–2014)	Too many delays	$559 million
Försäkringskassan Dental Health Service System (2007–2010)	Bad specifications	$1.18 billion
BBC Digital Media Initiative (2008–2013)	Bad specifications	$134 million
Surrey Integrated Reporting Enterprise Network (2009–2013)	Bad specifications	$20 million
Pust Siebel Policy Case Management (2011–2014)	Did not function	$35 million
Cover Oregon (2012–2014)	Did not function	$200 million

Opportunity Costs

Opportunity costs are benefits given up by choosing one alternative over another. For example, if an organization chooses to build a blog framework from scratch instead of using Webflow or WordPress, the developer time spent building the blog framework is an opportunity cost that could have been spent building something else. (Moreover, the likelihood that an organization will build a blog framework that is anywhere near as good as Webflow or WordPress is very low; those organizations have a core competency in building blog frameworks, whereas the average organization does not.) Additionally, the cost of maintaining that blog framework (to the extent that it requires more developer time than maintaining the third-party alternative) is also an opportunity cost. Many executives find that opportunity costs are the most overlooked cost of building over buying yet another piece of software inside an organization.

The primary opportunity costs in software development are labor costs: Choosing to run servers on-premises has an opportunity cost over public cloud in the additional personnel needed internally. Choosing to build over buy has an opportunity cost in the personnel needed to do the building. Opportunity costs should be calculated as an estimate between alternatives.

Indirect Costs

Indirect costs in software development are those that are necessary to build and run software but are not attributed directly to the software project itself. For example, electricity and Internet access are both indirect costs for most software projects. These are usually not an important part of comparing alternative choices for building software because indirect costs tend to be much smaller in size than other costs and do not tend to vary between alternatives.

Fixed Costs

Fixed costs are like direct costs, with an exception: Fixed costs are paid for by the organization and used across projects, whereas direct costs are incurred for the specific project itself. Another key characteristic of fixed costs is that they do not vary with the number of customers or users of the software. For example, up-front labor on a project is a direct cost, but physical infrastructure used across the company is a fixed cost.

The largest category of fixed costs that are specific to software development (not including considerations such as office space or marketing) tends to be for the infrastructure, services, and libraries that are necessary to develop, build, test, and run the software and that are not billed on a per-use basis. These tend to get much more focus in organizations than direct costs (especially labor)—for example, with a multitude of services that will help companies reduce their cloud bills. If an organization is spending $1.5 million on developers and $5,000 per month on licensing a library, more people tend to be thinking and talking about reducing the licensing bill than reducing the cost of developers.

The best way to reduce these fixed costs is to use Serverless architectures, in which organizations pay only for value, not for reserving specific resources. In doing so, these could become direct costs because, in a Serverless architecture, the managed services being purchased are specific to the application (as with a text-messaging service), not the infrastructure (as with a virtual machine). Chapter 5, "Introducing Branch," dives into more detail on how Branch, which is Serverless, spends much less but has a more robust infrastructure than a typical enterprise.

Variable Costs

Variable costs in software change with the number of customers. Before the advent of software delivery over the Internet, the primary variable costs in software were packaging: CDs, DVDs, boxes, and manuals. Today, most variable costs are infrastructure costs needed when scaling. They are usually insignificant relative to the value of having those customers because software margins are so high (the median margin on software is around 75%).

However, variable costs can be brutally high for software in two main situations: (1) when there is no working monetization strategy (for example, the software is free for the high number of users but the provider makes no money) and (2) when the architecture of the application leads to underlying variable infrastructure costs that are surprisingly high per customer. The former case is not particularly interesting from a cost analysis perspective, except to say that if an organization cannot find a way to generate revenue effectively, no costs will be acceptable. The latter case is more avoidable and requires organizations to understand how they are charged by their infrastructure providers and what infrastructure is required per customer. Chapter 4, "Serverless Objections, Serverless Success," examines how to avoid these situations when it discusses common objections to Serverless.

Sunk Costs

Sunk costs are those that have already been incurred and cannot be undone. Identifying sunk costs and explicitly keeping them out of comparisons is useful because these costs do not matter to a forward-looking view of costs. For example, if an organization has already spent millions of dollars developing software that is functional but has a massive amount of technical debt, it's not important to worry about the millions already spent in determining the right choice going forward.

Controllable Costs

Controllable costs are short-term costs that are determined by an individual, such as the general manager of a software development project. Examples of controllable costs are bonuses, team meals, and other items that should not have a significant impact on comparing software development alternatives.

Undifferentiated Heavy Lifting

One of the best ways to eliminate unnecessary costs in software development projects is to identify what elements of the project are undifferentiated heavy lifting. *Undifferentiated* means that it is not a core part of how the company is trying to win in the marketplace. In other words, the customers of the software do not care how the organization accomplishes the element—whether it is done in-house or by a third party, or how it is implemented by whoever does it. *Heavy lifting* means that it may have substantial direct, fixed, variable, and/or opportunity costs.

One example of undifferentiated heavy lifting is generating electricity. Clearly, electricity is necessary to power the computers upon which software runs. With SaaS, the software provider must have its own electricity to run the software. However, the end users of software likely do not care whether the software provider is running its own power plant, purchasing power from a local electric company (perhaps with generator backup), or running its software on a cloud service provider that handles all electrical provider decision-making.

One increasingly less controversial example of undifferentiated heavy lifting is running software on-premises or in a colocation facility instead of using a public cloud provider. Customers care about their software being available and fast; however, they do not care where the servers are located, beyond perhaps wanting all of them to be within a certain country or countries for regulatory or security reasons.

Much of this book helps explain why the category of undifferentiated heavy lifting is much bigger than most software developers and architects think. After finishing this book, business and technology leaders alike should have the tools and knowledge to classify which elements of their software projects must be highly controlled and custom built and which need not be.

Code Is a Liability

One of the biggest mistakes organizations make in thinking about the software they build is viewing the source code written as an asset. That may make some intuitive sense: Here is a proprietary set of instructions that, when executed, generates revenue for us! Eric Lee, a senior software engineer at Microsoft, explains that code is much more like debt:[4]

> "Source code is akin to financial debt. Suppose you want to buy a house to live in. Most people do not have the financial wherewithal to pay cash for a house, so you take out a mortgage instead. The mortgage is the instrument that allows you to have a house to live in. But the mortgage itself is not a great thing to have. It is a liability. You must pay interest on your debt every month. You always want your mortgage to be as small as possible while still allowing you to buy a house that meets your needs."

Unnecessarily repetitive and bad code is known as technical debt. Most forward-thinking software developers seek to avoid it and pay it down because technical debt is a liability. Replacing unnecessarily duplicative and bad code almost always results in having less code to maintain. In addition, all code requires continuing investment, no matter how well written it is.

However, the position that organizations should seek to minimize the amount of overall code that they write and maintain can be controversial, because senior developers often see code that was intentionally written to use fewer lines but is unmaintainable. What matters is *maintainability*; generally, less code is more maintainable, but not less code to an absurd level.

Another argument offered against broadly minimizing the amount of code written and maintained is that if an organization has less code, it has less intellectual property and, therefore, less of a moat. This argument does not stand up under scrutiny. If two organizations have equivalent SaaS products, but one has 2 million lines of code and the other has 10,000 lines of code, no market is going to value the former more—if anything, the product with the longer code would have lesser value because the alternative product is likely operating with faster development velocity and smaller teams. An organization might need to write code to implement critical intellectual property (such as a patent or trade secret), but the actual code itself is not inherently valuable as anything other than the tactical implementation.

The essential point to understand about code is that it is a means to an end; the easier code is to maintain, the less of a liability it is. Organizations should seek to optimize for the maintainability of their code base: What is the velocity of developers working within the code base? How long does it take a new developer to become productive? How much nondevelopment support staff does it take to develop, deploy, run, and maintain the software? Chapter 8, "Getting to Serverless," examines these and more relevant metrics in detail. For this chapter, the important takeaway is that code is a liability.

The Experience Is the Asset

If the code is a liability, what exactly is the asset in software development? The asset is the solution to the problem that the software solves for its users and the value of solving that problem. This should not be a controversial statement, but unfortunately, many software developers put their pride into what they have built, not necessarily in the user experience and value it delivers (see Figure 2.2).

Although hard work should be celebrated, what developers build is less important to the overall mission of an organization than the value it delivers. Given the rapid pace of technology, it is not uncommon to find that, several years after building something, plenty of bespoke code is better replaced with standard libraries or services than maintained forever.

Technologists also offer bad, impulsive arguments in the guise of defending customer experience, but these are really just defenses of desired technical implementations. Speed is an important aspect of almost all software, but it is important to determine whether an overemphasis on unnecessary speed is driving poor decisions from an organizational perspective. For example, high-frequency trading applications can require speed that forces them to be deployed physically in specific data centers so that they can make trades 1 or 2 milliseconds faster than other applications. On the other hand, a web application used in the back office of small or medium-size businesses (for example, dental practice management software) is probably fine if most pages load in 2 seconds or less. Chapter 4 has more coverage of speed and other potential pretextual arguments for undifferentiated heavy lifting.

Figure 2.2 *A Developer Reveals, in Question Form, What Matters to Him (from Quora)*

Summary: How to Pick the Right Way to Build a Software Project

The tools in this chapter help teams pick the best ways to design, build, deploy, run, and maintain software. When faced with a series of alternative software architectures, the primary question to ask is whether the right customer experience can be implemented in each of the different architectures. Alternatives that cannot reasonably meet customer experience needs should not be considered.

After gathering the possible designs, the organization should analyze the complete costs of each alternative. Some specific points to think about follow:

- Which alternatives are likely to be easiest to change and maintain over time, given that more code is a liability?

- Which alternatives are most likely to have underestimated direct costs because of a larger amount of bespoke work done in-house?

- Which alternatives allow for a faster launch to market, enabling work to address bugs, usability, and feature issues to start sooner?

- Which alternatives will have lower fixed costs due to paying for services based upon value (in Serverless architectures)?

- What will the variable costs be under different usage scenarios?

- Which alternatives do opportunity costs favor?

References

[1] "What Are Different Types of Cost Accounting?" www.investopedia.com/ask/answers/041415/what-are-different-types-costs-cost-accounting.asp

[2] Emison, Joe. "Software Development: It's Not Like Construction." (2016) https://thenewstack.io/modern-effective-software-development-15/

[3] "List of Failed and Overbudget Custom Software Projects." https://en.wikipedia.org/wiki/List_of_failed_and_overbudget_custom_software_projects

[4] Lee, Eric. "Source Code Is a Liability, Not an Asset." (2009) https://saintgimp.org/2009/03/11/source-code-is-a-liability-not-an-asset/

Chapter 3

Serverless Architectures

This chapter explains why software designs with Serverless elements are usually superior to designs without those elements. However, before discussing Serverless design, it is useful to look at the philosophy Amazon has used to become dominant in commerce and cloud computing; it is a very similar philosophy to building Serverless applications. This chapter then defines what Serverless is and explains how front ends, back ends, functions, and managed services all fit into the larger Serverless picture.

The Amazon Way

Steve Yegge, an engineer who worked at Amazon in its infancy, re-created from his memory a memo that Jeff Bezos sent to all Amazon employees in 2002.

How Amazon Builds

By Steve Yegge

[Quite a few years ago,] Jeff Bezos issued a mandate [that] went something along these lines:

1. All teams will henceforth expose their data and functionality through service interfaces.

2. Teams must communicate with each other through these interfaces.

---

3. There will be no other form of interprocess communication allowed: no direct linking, no direct reads of another team's datastore, no shared-memory model, no back-doors whatsoever. The only communication allowed is via service interface calls over the network.

4. It doesn't matter what technology they use. HTTP, CORBA, Pubsub, custom protocols—doesn't matter. Bezos doesn't care.

5. All service interfaces, without exception, must be designed from the ground up to be externalizable. That is to say, the team must plan and design to be able to expose the interface to developers in the outside world. No exceptions.

6. Anyone who doesn't do this will be fired.

[After Bezos sent out that memo, over] the next couple of years, Amazon transformed internally into a service-oriented architecture. They learned a tremendous amount while effecting this transformation. There was lots of existing documentation and lore about SOAs, but at Amazon's vast scale, it was about as useful as telling Indiana Jones to look both ways before crossing the street. Amazon's dev staff made a lot of discoveries along the way. A teeny tiny sampling of these discoveries included:

- Pager escalation gets way harder because a ticket might bounce through 20 service calls before the real owner is identified. If each bounce goes through a team with a 15-minute response time, it can be hours before the right team finally finds out, unless you build a lot of scaffolding and metrics and reporting.

- Every single one of your peer teams suddenly becomes a potential DOS [denial of service] attacker. Nobody can make any real forward progress until very serious quotas and throttling are put in place in every single service.

- Monitoring and QA are the same thing. You'd never think so until you try doing a big SOA. But when your service says, "Oh yes, I'm fine," it may well be the case that the only thing still functioning in the server is the little component that knows how to say "I'm fine, roger roger, over and out" in a cheery droid voice. To tell whether the service is actually responding, you have to make individual calls. The problem continues recursively until your monitoring is doing comprehensive semantics checking of your entire range of services and data, at which point it is indistinguishable from automated QA. So they're a continuum.

- If you have hundreds of services, and your code *must* communicate with other groups' code via these services, then you won't be able to find any of them without a service-discovery mechanism. And you can't have that without a service registration mechanism, which itself is another service. So Amazon has a universal service registry where you can find out reflectively (programmatically) about every service, what its APIs are, and also whether it is currently up and where.

- Debugging problems with someone else's code gets a *lot* harder and is basically impossible unless there is a universal standard way to run every service in a debuggable sandbox.

That's just a very small sample. There are dozens, maybe hundreds, of individual learnings like these that Amazon had to discover organically. There were a lot of wacky ones around externalizing services, but not as many as you might think. Organizing into services taught teams not to trust each other in most of the same ways they're not supposed to trust external developers.

Amazon's internal departments and teams have much greater autonomy than teams in the average organization. Each Amazon team treats other teams as if they are external third parties. Teams cannot order each other around, and, by and large, executives cannot force teams to build things that they do not themselves believe create value for the teams' customers. Thus, teams control their own roadmaps while effectively using other AWS services, without having to coordinate with those teams in a special way.

This attitude can be applied by any organization, small or large, by including all the SaaS and APIs available in the world today. Every service that an organization can embed in its own applications via API (think Twilio), and every SaaS that enables an organization to deliver a particular customer experience (think Zendesk) is like having a department full of designers, developers, and operators that interacts with teams the way that Amazon interacts internally.

The key lesson from Amazon, which has helped define so much of what is considered Serverless today, is that the only way for organizations to build quickly and effectively is to have small, decentralized teams with common interfaces. The magic of Serverless is that, instead of having to build those teams internally in an organization, organizations can simply buy services that function as departments or divisions for them. Just as an organization pays the power company for power, an organization can pay for services that do the work of an entire department (such as payroll implementation) or the work of part of an application (such as searching full text within a database or making thumbnail images). These services make it much easier to build the next Amazon. The rest of this chapter explains in detail how to think about building software the same way.

What Is Serverless?

Throughout this book, the term *Serverless* is used to describe a way to develop, build, deliver, and maintain software. Many people hate the term, for various reasons. There are, of course, still servers somewhere, much as there are still wires involved when you use wireless technology. Furthermore, most original Serverless applications used a very narrow set of the full range of Serverless tools—Functions as a Service—so that original narrow view has incorrectly carried into many people's current understandings of Serverless. Ultimately, the term itself is fine, but different people learn different ways; this book thus presents several different definitions of *Serverless*, from strategic to technically detailed, so that all readers can pick their own preferred choice.

Serverless Is a Focus on Business Value

Ben Kehoe, an AWS Serverless Hero and formerly a cloud robotics research scientist at iRobot, writes and speaks about the Serverless Mindset, which he summarizes in this way:[1]

> "Serverless is a way to focus on business value.
>
> How [does writing Serverless applications] help you deliver value? [It] lets you focus on writing business logic, not coding supporting infrastructure for your business logic.
>
> Managed services let you focus on writing your functions. Having [fewer] operations resources frees up people and money to be applied to creating new value for your customers....
>
> You should go Serverless because you want to focus on creating value—and at your company, you endeavor to apply technology toward the creation of business value."

Ben's definition is a nice addition to the first two because it supplies the motivation for Serverless. In building a Serverless application, the outcome should be a much greater focus on business value and a reduction in distractions (especially undifferentiated heavy lifting). The Serverless Mindset, as he describes it, is one that is constantly searching for ways to increase focus on what matters.

Serverless Means Not Our Uptime

One of the simplest definitions of Serverless, and the principal way I think about fully Serverless applications, is that the responsibility for keeping applications running is not the responsibility of the organization that developed the applications. Managed service providers handle all infrastructure, operating system, and system software planning, procurement, deployment, patching, failover, and scaling. An organization develops and configures its application and then provides the necessary code, binaries, and configuration to managed service providers to handle everything else.

Note that standard cloud Infrastructure-as-a-Service (IaaS) and Platform-as-a-Service (PaaS) services are not Serverless by the "not our uptime" definition because organizations have to own failure scenarios with those cloud infrastructure options. For example, even managed database services that have some level of automated failover don't have ways of automatically handling problems, from running out of disk space to being overwhelmed by too much traffic. One good way to tell whether an organization is still responsible for some uptime is to walk through disaster recovery and business continuity plans and see where technical skills are required; anything that involves DNS, load balancers, or run books indicates that an essential part of uptime is still managed within the organization.

Sometimes executives think about Serverless as being just one step further on a path to outsource more to managed-service providers. To some extent, this is true, but Serverless is also the last step, and that is significant.

Think about vaccinations as an approach to mitigating disease risk: Perhaps being vaccinated in round 1 reduces the risk of contracting a particular disease from a 2% likelihood to a 1% likelihood. Now contrast that with how you would feel if you could further take that risk from 1% to 0% with perhaps a second round of vaccination, and you get a sense of how Serverless differs from the cloud outsourcing that came before it. In both the 2–1% reduction and 1–0% reduction, exactly the same absolute risk reduction is achieved. But after the second step, you are freed in a way that you never were before, to the point that you no longer face any risk of getting the disease. In the case of Serverless, the "disease" is having to maintain skills and staff to handle infrastructure management, including continuous monitoring and failure handling, which are all now undifferentiated tasks.

One of the simplest examples of a Serverless application from a "not our uptime" perspective is any store built on Shopify[2] (which, as with major cloud providers, does not run on a Serverless architecture but enables others to run Serverlessly). Shopify allows anyone to build a complete, customized e-commerce web application that Shopify runs entirely. A much more complex one is the software that runs the full-stack insurance company Branch; it is explained in detail in Chapter 5, "Introducing Branch."

Four Technical Criteria for Serverless

Rob Sutter, a developer advocate at Amazon Web Services, has a useful four-criteria definition of Serverless:[3]

1. No infrastructure provisioning or management

2. Automatic scaling

3. Pay for value

4. Highly available and secure

This is more specific than "not our uptime," which helps clarify the value of Serverless and also excludes some criteria that might be marketed as Serverless but are not. It is useful to walk through several examples.

Infrastructure Provisioning

A Serverless managed service does not allow provisioning a specific infrastructure, nor does it require any management of infrastructure (see Figure 3.1). For example, most major cloud providers provide managed database services (such as AWS Relational Database Service), wherein the provider manages some functions of the database; however, these are almost always not Serverless. It's possible to tell that they are not Serverless because specific infrastructure choices must be made to deploy them: (How many different virtual machines? How many CPUs/cores on each virtual machine?) Additionally, when it comes time to apply a security patch or restore from a backup, the customer, not the provider, must decide when to do it. Perhaps worst, in the case of a customer's database going down, the customer must be monitoring the database and bring it back up. In contrast, in a handful of Serverless database services available, such as DynamoDB (AWS), CosmosDB (Azure), and Google Cloud Datastore, customers have no idea how many virtual machines or servers are running and do no management of the underlying database service.

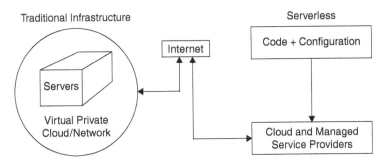

Figure 3.1 *Infrastructure Provisioning: Traditional vs. Serverless*

The Gray Area of Serverless Infrastructure Provisioning

Despite the focus on not provisioning infrastructure in a Serverless application, most Serverless compute platforms—often called Functions-as-a-Service (FaaS)—do allow for specifying how much memory will be allocated to run the function. Additionally, specifying the amount of memory often has an impact on how many CPUs or cores will be allocated to run the workload. Taken in the strictest sense, this is a violation of the "no infrastructure provisioning" criteria for Serverless; however, it is better seen as a way to control costs by exposing a very simple aspect of infrastructure provisioning as a configuration option.

More important, the aspect of infrastructure provisioning that causes so much operational pain and undifferentiated heavy lifting in organizations is the number of virtual machines and containers and the approach to spreading the workload across them. Specifying the amount of memory that will be allocated to run code is magnitudes simpler than having to worry about the number of different servers that must be provisioned and shut down to run the code.

Automatic Scaling

A Serverless application automatically scales through the managed services that it uses without needing any autoscaling rules set by its developers or operations staff to respond to increases or decreases in use. Scaling a typical managed SQL Server or MySQL database service at a cloud provider requires launching new servers, whereas scaling a Serverless database service can be handled automatically by the provider (see Figure 3.2). Google's Cloud Datastore has always autoscaled to whatever request load is sent to it. CosmosDB and DynamoDB have ways of limiting how quickly they respond to requests, to control costs, but both have added features in the past few years to automatically scale up and down in response to the real-time request load.

Pay for Value

In the early 2000s, companies had to purchase their own physical hardware to run web applications. One of the most exciting and disruptive aspects of the public cloud was that it allowed anyone to rent physical hardware by the hour (or even smaller time units). Although this was an enormous improvement for people building scalable, highly available software, it still required capacity planning (What kind of hardware do I need?) and resulted in organizations paying a lot of money for idle and underused infrastructure.

Serverless managed services have fine-grained billing that closely matches the value their services deliver because they can optimize capacity much more easily in their multitenant services. This means that, instead of paying for a certain number of CPU cores, memory, and hard drive space (typical SQL Server/MySQL managed database service pricing), a Serverless database service can charge based upon request volume—how often the database is being read and written by clients (see Figure 3.3).

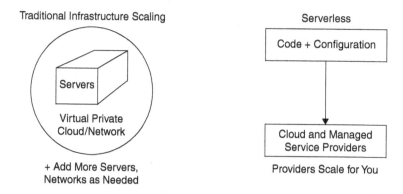

Figure 3.2 *Automatic Scaling: Traditional vs. Serverless*

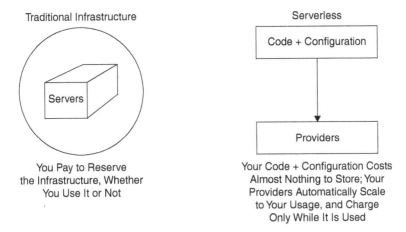

Figure 3.3 *Cost: Traditional vs. Serverless*

Highly Available and Secure

Finally, if an organization is going to hand off the responsibility of uptime, scaling, and failover to a managed service provider, that provider must provide a highly available service with adequate security. Without either of those two criteria, integrating the service into an application is not an acceptable decision. The database examples used throughout this section all have had excellent availability in practice and include best practices security as a central feature (see Figure 3.4).

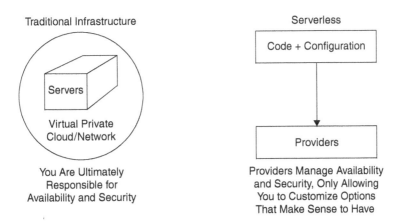

Figure 3.4 *Availability and Security: Traditional vs. Serverless*

Parts of Serverless Applications

Both Serverless and non-Serverless applications are made up of several components. But unlike a non-Serverless application, which might have its architecture described in terms of infrastructure (for example, a three-tier application), Serverless applications are defined in terms of

- Managed services
- Front ends
- Back ends
- Functions

Each of these can (but do not have to) involve some custom code, and each piece usually speaks to the other pieces through application programming interfaces (APIs).

Managed Services

The most important components of a Serverless application are managed services. Managed services are used by many, if not most, non-Serverless applications, and they are a wonderful gateway to making applications more Serverless. To make things confusing, there are non-Serverless managed services as well, and those do not help in building Serverless applications. Managed services can be low level and not application specific (for example, message queues or storage) or can be extremely high level and very domain specific (for example, AWS Elemental or Ground Station).

A Serverless managed service is one that runs infrastructure on behalf of its customers, automatically scales, charges for value, and is highly available and secure. It handles part of the functionality of your application that is undifferentiated from other applications—for example, how you send text messages to clients, how you resize images, or how you generate PDFs. The managed services allow you to focus on the content of the messages, images, and PDFs instead of the plumbing needed to make them.

It's also possible to think of the managed services in an application as the APIs that the application uses. Some APIs are called by the front end, other APIs are called by functions in the back end, and still other APIs call APIs. Finding all the managed services out in the world that developers can leverage to build better applications can be a full-time job. The appendixes and the companion website to this book provide a comprehensive directory to help organizations on their Serverless journey.

Front Ends

The front end of an application is the user interface. This can be an app on a smartphone, a web application running in a browser, a simple static web page viewed in a browser, or even a command-line interface. The code in a front end runs on client devices (smartphones, web browsers, and computers) and thus does not require any servers in its execution. However, it is necessary to have some location where users can download the front end so that they can run it on their device. For smartphone apps, this is usually an app store, but for web applications, developers must have a host for their front ends. Lots of organizations already use Serverless managed services to host their front ends, such as AWS Simple Storage Service (S3, one of the first public cloud services released, in 2006), or its comparable services on other providers, as well as through content delivery networks (CDNs).

One of the more popular Serverless application architecture movements is the JAMstack[4] (JavaScript, APIs, and markup), which seeks to put all necessary business logic into the front end of an application and to rely upon managed services through APIs to handle any back-end logic, without needing a back end. Many great examples of JAMstack sites exist, including covidtracking.com, but it is not necessary to completely avoid building back ends to be Serverless.

Back Ends and Functions

The most complicated and least well understood elements of Serverless applications are back ends and functions, which are best thought of as the functionality necessary for the front end to work properly. For example, in an application that supports booking hotel rooms, the back end needs to be able to search various providers of hotel rooms, retrieve prices, make bookings, and bill credit cards.

The biggest initial challenge with Serverless back ends is security. When front-end code is running on a client device, it cannot be trusted because the user can examine what it is doing and try to manipulate it. This need to have low trust in front-end code has always been a major reason why software architects and developers have wanted to keep tight control over application authentication and custom-code data access in the back end for SaaS. For example, an application that allows users to take and send pictures, such as Snapchat, needs to make sure that the front-end application it provides to users cannot access pictures that the user was not given access to.[5]

Two companies, Parse (mentioned in the Introduction) and Firebase, came up with good but different solutions to the need to provide low trust access to Serverless back ends. Separately, each company built a Serverless database with user sign-up and authentication features and access control rules that could be set by configuration across all users. This allowed developers to build front-end applications that allowed the users to use their own identities (email address and user-defined password) to sign up for accounts and log into accounts with the back end, yet be limited to only what they were allowed to access. In addition, Parse provided a way for developers to write small, custom code (cloud code) that would run safely in the back end to handle processes that could not be trusted in the front end, such as billing credit cards.

As the first versions of this new Serverless paradigm for back ends, however, these Backends-as-a-Service (BaaS) had several limitations and annoyances: The Parse security rule system was extremely painful at scale, neither Parse nor Firebase datastores worked all that well for data shared among many users, and it was not clear how to build many types of applications successfully with their services. But instead of taking significant steps to fix these (and other) issues, Facebook shut down Parse, and Google Cloud acquired Firebase and refocused its teams' development efforts on other efforts (such as giving Google better mobile application development support).

The next step taken in Serverless back-end architectures was both a bit of a step back and a reformulation of what Serverless back ends should be. In 2014 and 2015, Amazon Web Services launched its Lambda and API Gateway services. Lambda runs custom code without having to provision or operate infrastructure (Functions-as-a-Service [FaaS]). API Gateway allows calling Lambda functions and other Amazon Services through the Internet, although Amazon has now added functionality to call Lambda functions directly without using API Gateway. These two services together allowed custom code to be run Serverlessly. They also facilitated, through the custom-coded functions running on AWS Lambda, the ability to write any application at all.

However, at the beginning, it was not clear what was the best way to architect applications that had back ends running on FaaS. Many of the initial application architectures did not make good on the Serverless promise of being easier to maintain. Applications were divided into many functions, so application architects often made too many different functions—in some cases, putting every single application function into its own Lambda (see Figure 3.5). This approach makes applications hard to develop and maintain and can cause a lot of unintended consequences, especially when functions call other functions (for example, infinite loops leading to infinite cost).[6]

Many applications have been built on Lambda and API Gateway, including A Cloud Guru's cloud training platform (see the references at the end of this chapter for a great talk by Sam Kroonenburg, the CEO and architect of their application).[7]

In the past few years, fantastic new back-end services have launched that have improved upon the original Parse capabilities of authentication + access control + database + custom code functions. AWS has its Amplify ecosystem, which is a set

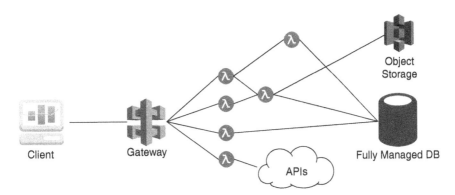

Figure 3.5 *A Functions-as-a-Service (FaaS) Serverless Back End*

of libraries and services (including Lambda) that allows front-end developers to build Serverless applications with many AWS services through a simple command-line interface and web console. Google has continued to improve Firebase, adding functions, new datastores, and many mobile app–specific features. Netlify, a front-end hosting service, has added authentication, function, and database capabilities (the latter through Serverless Database-as-a-Service FaunaDB).[8] Even more great Serverless back-end services are available, including Prisma, discussed in more detail in Part IV.[9, 10]

Summary: What Is Serverless?

This chapter explains Serverless architectures by starting with the organizational philosophy that helped Amazon become a global juggernaut in commerce and cloud computing. Building a Serverless application is a lot like building new products within Amazon: The approach leverages managed services (departments) via scalable interfaces (APIs) so that all that needs to be built anew are the differentiated parts of the applications.

With that as a framework, this chapter gives several different ways to think about the core criteria of Serverless, culminating in a four-criteria definition: no infrastructure management, automatic scaling, pay for value, and highly available and secure. Finally, the chapter walks through the key components of a Serverless application.

References

[1] "Serverless is a State of Mind." https://ben11kehoe.medium.com/serverless-is-a-state-of-mind-717ef2088b42

[2] "Start selling with Shopify today." www.shopify.com/blog/start-online-store

[3] "Go Serverless! Stop worrying about infrastructure and ship more." https://speakerdeck.com/robsutter/go-serverless-stop-worrying-about-infrastructure-and-ship-more

[4] "What is Jamstack?" https://jamstack.org/

[5] "Snapchat API Hack: What Happened?" www.akana.com/blog/snapchat-api-hack

[6] "The Serverless Sea Change." www.infoq.com/articles/serverless-sea-change/

[7] "From One Function to 43 Microservices" free login. https://acloud.guru/series/serverlessconf-nyc-2019/view/from-one-to-43

[8] "Announcing the FaunaDB Add-on for Netlify." www.netlify.com/blog/2019/09/10/announcing-the-faunadb-add-on-for-netlify/

[9] "The Happy Demise of the 10X Engineer." https://a16z.com/2014/07/30/the-happy-demise-of-the-10x-engineer/

[10] "Full-Stack Development in the Era of Serverless Computing." https://medium.com/@dabit3/full-stack-development-in-the-era-of-serverless-computing-c1e49bba8580

Chapter 4

Serverless Objections, Serverless Success

Embracing Serverless architectures is controversial within most organizations because so much of what organizations have thus far done internally will be delegated to external providers going forward. People who have built their careers and identities around expertise that an organization no longer needs are highly motivated to identify any rational reasons to halt a move to Serverless. This chapter walks through many of the common objections to Serverless and explains why they generally are not legitimate reasons to hold back. It also highlights several success stories that are good counterexamples to the fear, uncertainty, and doubt that Serverless objectors seek to create.

Loss of Control

The most important and painful obstacle to running a Serverless architecture is that an organization gives up the control to restore functionality, especially during an incident. This cannot be underemphasized. I recommend that you flag this section of the book so that you can reread it when you experience an outage that you cannot control because you chose to go Serverless. Nothing is worse than being unable to do anything to bring your service back up. Nothing will challenge a strategy to go Serverless more than wanting to own uptime so that it's possible to fix an outage using internal staff.

The problem with owning uptime, however, is twofold: Statistically, organizations do not achieve better uptime by having more control over it, and owning uptime is also significantly more expensive. Thus, over time and at scale, owning uptime offers a terrible return on investment. But it often can feel like the right decision in the rare moment that an organization is stuck waiting on a vendor.

One of the best ways to understand the weakness of the arguments for more control over uptime is that, if it were truly the case that organizations need to have better control, every company should still be generating its own electricity, and every "as-a-Service" offering would be a poor business decision. Thus, organizations can ask a better, more nuanced question about when it makes sense to give up control: Under what circumstances would a transfer of control to a vendor be a poor decision?

Businesses regularly transfer uptime control to vendors for other technical services. Consider what happens when Slack, Zoom, or Microsoft Office 365 becomes unavailable: Organizations wait for them to come back online, which usually happens quickly. This transfer of control should be problematic only if the vendor does a significantly worse job of keeping its services running or restoring them after incidents than organizations would themselves.

Most managed-service providers run their services more effectively and with less downtime than their clients will run those same services. This is because those providers know the services better, and keeping them up is their primary responsibility. Additionally, because they are operating the same service for many organizations, they can learn, at scale, many more potential areas for operational failure than any individual organization could learn on its own in the same time frame. Most vendors also have status/health pages with historical data to review their operating histories, so it is possible to understand historical uptime before purchase. If a vendor does not have a status/health page, that is a sign that perhaps the vendor is not yet ready to support important use cases.

Other aspects of transfers of control to vendors in Serverless architectures are important to consider, such as having to adopt a vendor's unique method of interaction (for example, a vendor might require XML, and the rest of the application might use only JSON) or way of thinking about their service. Vendors might also force upgrades, such as runtimes for Serverless functions, so an organization might have to modify code to be compatible with newer versions. Information security concerns can also arise, as discussed in more detail later in this chapter.

But in all cases, the gains that Serverless architectures provide necessarily result in some loss of control. That loss of control is good—it drives the organizational agility and speed benefits that Serverless delivers. In some cases, the loss of control is not acceptable, but that determination should be made only after a rational evaluation of pros and cons. In that evaluation, it can be helpful to think about a given vendor's choices in how its service works as being the more than acceptable price of its assumption of responsibility. In other words, if a vendor's API or documentation or architecture seems odd, that should not necessarily be a valid reason not to use the vendor. On the other hand, if a vendor's historical uptime or security practices are unacceptable, that is a deal breaker.

Other Common Objections

Lock-In

The most common objection to Serverless application architectures is that they lead to lock-in. Lock-in is shorthand for the notion that an organization will be held hostage to the vendors being used, leading to extreme costs, unexpected downtime, and/or an inability to make changes in the future because of an essentially unbreakable reliance upon those vendors. However, the lock-in objection rarely makes rational sense as a reason not to implement Serverless architectures or managed services. This section explains why.

History

It is worthwhile to understand how lock-in objection originated: with database software. Oracle perhaps most notoriously took advantage of how software developers used proprietary aspects of databases to continue increasing its database licensing prices while companies had impossibly high switching costs. (But really, this was true of every database vendor.) Oracle's notoriety here comes from its extremely high prices relative to potential alternatives (for example, $5,000 per CPU per computer running Oracle, compared to no licensing cost for MySQL or PostgreSQL) and its regular auditing of customers to find every place Oracle software was in use.[1] VMware and Microsoft are also well known for creating a cottage industry of lawyers who specialize in helping companies push back against audits.[2]

Understandably, the feelings of helplessness and anger in response to technology vendors charging increasingly higher prices for software that companies rely upon have led to incessant worry over future lock-in. However, these worries are rarely properly evaluated against how likely a particular choice is to lead to a bad outcome. Note that no major cloud provider has a track record of raising costs as a policy to generate more revenue. Instead, the worries are vague and tend to take a negative view of any situation in which a vendor has a unique product that will incur some switching costs.

A Lock-In Analysis Framework

Gregor Hohpe, a writer at ArchitectElevator.com, has a useful framework for evaluating lock-in: How unique is the utility, and how high is the switching cost?[3] If the utility is unique and the switching costs are low, the choice is easy: Do it. It might seem contradictory that a utility could be unique with low switching costs, so an example helps here. Twilio is unique as an SMS service because it has more integrations with other service providers, and developers are generally more familiar with it than any of its competitors. Switching from Twilio to another provider would require porting numbers and potentially custom-writing some new integrations, but overall, the switching cost is low; organizations stay with Twilio for its uniqueness, not because of its high switching costs.

If the utility is not unique and the switching costs are high, this is like the database situation mentioned earlier: Think about lock-in ahead of time, and make a choice with that consideration in mind. If the utility is unique and the switching costs are high, this is likely an acceptable situation for lock-in; organizations should be willing to pay for unique utility.

Serverless architectures, as they are featured in this book, are fundamentally about using managed-service providers to implement common features of applications: authentication, static asset hosting, image resizing, caching, and search. Instead of being outsourced to vendors, these services have almost always been developed and run in-house. But under a Serverless architecture, an organization can choose to handle something like image resizing through a service such as Cloudinary, which takes almost no time to implement, or by running and orchestrating an open-source library such as Imagemagick itself.[4] In all these cases, the switching costs are very small: Moving from Cloudinary to Imagemagick simply requires orchestrating Imagemagick, which is a far cry from converting a large application from one proprietary database to another.

Said another way, the managed services that underpin Serverless applications can be seen as faster and easier versions of "run-it-yourself" options for the same functionality that has been used for years. To build more quickly and focus on what matters, organizations can opt to use those managed services. If the organization gets upset at the managed-service provider in question at some point, the organization can choose to run that functionality itself, at the same cost it initially avoided by delegating that functionality.

A potentially complicating factor arises in calculating switching costs for managed services: data gravity. If an organization has been storing a significant amount of data with a managed-service provider, it is usually necessary to move that data as part of a switch, and sometimes large amounts of data can be difficult to move—hence, *gravity*. The good news is that most managed-service providers have simple APIs that allow for easy data portability; for example, Cloudinary has a fairly simple way to export all data.[5] In some managed services, exporting data is more difficult (for example, authentication providers such as AWS Cognito do not provide even encrypted password exports), but most providers make it possible to migrate to competing services (for example, Stripe helps organizations export data to another payment processor).[6] The biggest challenges with data gravity come at very large amounts of data (hundreds of petabytes of files in object storage, or billions of rows in databases), so if an organization has that immense volume of data, it is worth thinking through how migration might work.

Another aspect of Serverless architectures that can keep switching costs low is that Serverless architectures can use many different service providers instead of being monolithically reliant upon something like a single database vendor's software. Within a Serverless application, data can be spread to different providers instead of being stored only in one location (for example, a payments vendor holding card information, or images being stored and resized in a separate service). This offers multiple benefits: It keeps vendors from being able to extort higher prices because their value is contained to a particular function of the application, and it limits the scope of what needs to be migrated to only what that service provides. This is not to suggest that an organization should optimize for many different service providers; instead, by seeking the best managed services, organizations with Serverless architectures will naturally have more vendor heterogeneity.

Performance and Cold Starts

Delegating operating responsibility to vendors in Serverless architectures also means that those vendors will be responsible for performance. Many people who have dabbled with Functions-as-a-Service (FaaS), such as Lambda from Amazon Web Services, have seen that applications can suffer slower performance due to cold starts. A cold start is the first invocation of a function; it requires allocating infrastructure and is slower than subsequent invocations (dubbed warm starts), often by a second or more.

The good news about performance is twofold: First, most vendors are highly attuned to the performance of their services and generally deliver better performance than non-Serverless alternatives. For example, the Algolia Serverless search index service usually returns results in less than one-tenth the time that the Elasticsearch service does. Second, even when the default behavior might be slower (as with cold starts), vendors offer the option to pay more for better performance (as with Amazon's Provisioned Concurrency for Lambda Functions).[7]

In a small minority of niche cases, a managed service is not performant enough and requires running a bespoke solution. The poster child for this type of niche case is high-frequency trading: Each millisecond gained in speed can be meaningful, and it pays to locate code in data centers that are physically closer to the source of truth. In most real-world software development, however, managed services should meet the desired performance needs.

Security, Especially in Multitenancy

The final common category of objection to Serverless architectures revolves around security. Any time information is being sent to third parties, potential security concerns arise. Additionally, most managed service providers are multitenant, meaning that the vendor uses the same physical infrastructure to store multiple customers' information. To the extent that an organization stores information that must be stored and transferred in particular ways, it is critical to ensure that all vendors that will have access to that information are compliant with the proper information security processes.

Managed-service providers increasingly cater to organizations that have significant, regulated information security needs. For example, Algolia[8] and Auth0[9] are compliant with the Health Insurance Portability and Accountability Act (HIPAA) and General Data Protection Regulation (GDPR), among other regulatory restrictions, provided that their customers hold up their shared responsibilities. Additionally, some providers allow organizations to outsource compliance pain, akin to how Stripe handles essentially all expensive aspects of Payment Card Industry Data Security Standards (PCI DSS) compliance.[10]

Before assessing vendors on their information security practices and appropriateness for use as part of an application, it is critical that organizations audit and classify their own information assets. For example, the requirements for storing information such as recipes that are in the public domain should be significantly different than personally identifiable information, such as customers' name, address, and date of birth. If an organization has well-defined information security, evaluating vendors should be straightforward.

Security is no longer an afterthought for companies running in the cloud. All serious vendors have System and Organization Controls (SOC) audits annually. These audits produce a significant amount of documentation that organizations can and should read in assessing whether a vendor is following the appropriate, necessary security measures.

Success Stories

iRobot[11]

iRobot makes Roomba robot vacuum cleaners, including "connected" Roombas that enable customers to drive the robots over the Internet. When iRobot looked at the different options for supporting its connected features, it saw a lot of requirements for expertise that it did not have: cloud infrastructure and cloud operations. iRobot's customers did not care whether iRobot had that expertise internally or whether iRobot outsourced it.

iRobot turned to Amazon Web Services and embraced several services that AWS had built to handle device/Internet of Things (IoT) use cases. iRobot did not have to worry about physical hardware, virtual hardware, capacity planning, or really anything beyond writing its code and telling AWS the hardware requirements for running the code (this is an oversimplification, but not insanely so). In 2018, Ben Kehoe, a cloud robotics research scientist at iRobot, described the company's Serverless applications as being more than 100 functions and "two dozen-ish AWS services," managed by 10 to 15 developers handling everything from development, to deployment, to incident management.

Another significant iRobot success story took place on Christmas 2021,[12] when, as Kehoe explains, "Everybody who has bought a Roomba since Black Friday opens them in about a 4-hour window on Christmas morning" (see Figure 4.1). What made Christmas 2021 especially amazing for iRobot is that no operations staff at iRobot had to do anything in response to the traffic spike. The chart shown here obscures how big the spike actually was because it's a daily traffic chart and doesn't show the concentration within the 4-hour period.

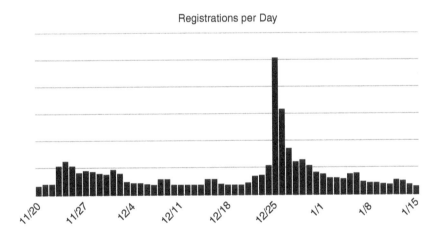

Figure 4.1 *iRobot Traffic Spikes on Christmas Day*

Lego[13, 14]

The LEGO.com website was migrated from a traditional monolithic codebase that ran on traditional servers to its current, fully Serverless architecture. The 10-month project was completed in July 2019. A primary driver for this move was the pain of spikes of traffic around releases and holidays, often leading to customers seeing only a maintenance page because the servers could not handle the traffic. LEGO was able to migrate its website in pieces, identifying the slowest elements of code that were most responsible for the performance bottlenecks and then rewriting them, one at a time, as Serverless functions that scale effortlessly.

LEGO has also found that it can make its application developers responsible for running their applications in production instead of only writing the code and relying on different personnel with different skills to run it. Serverless makes it possible to centralize the responsibility for development and operations with individuals, which, in turn, dramatically improves speed and stability.

The COVID Tracking Project[15]

In February 2020, Erin Kissane and others at *The Atlantic* launched a popular COVID tracking site at www.covidtracking.com/. The site scaled easily from nothing to two million API requests in three months because it was built Serverlessly. By using a headless content management system (CMS) and Google Sheets for editors to develop content, in conjunction with a static site generator and Netlify's static site hosting service, The COVID Tracking Project removed the need to generate anything on-demand.

This static site generation method even extended to the API, which consists of JSON files generated only when the Project receives enough new data. Those files are then made available as a static file for download for all.

It Is Just the Beginning

Many organizations have found early success in their initial forays into Serverless architectures—Coca-Cola, Edmunds, Fender, Comcast, Taco Bell, Liberty Mutual, AstraZeneca, and many more.[16] To date, most of the enterprise focus on Serverless tends to be on the specific benefits gained by using FaaS as an alternative to running servers, virtual machines, or containers. However, as Chapter 3, "Serverless Architectures," explained, the benefits of Serverless extend far beyond the back end—front ends and managed services deliver substantial value as well. Part II of the book, "Real-World Serverless," gives an in-depth comparison of Branch, a fully Serverless full-stack insurance company, and its enterprise foil.

Summary: Why or Why Not Serverless?

Adopting Serverless infrastructures often sparks debate within most organizations due to the shift of numerous in-house tasks to external vendors. Individuals whose professional identities have been rooted in skills that are no longer essential to the organization tend to actively find justifiable reasons to resist the transition to Serverless. This chapter discussed several typical concerns associated with Serverless, such as loss of control, vendor lock-in, performance issues, and security risks, and dispels them as generally unwarranted grounds for resistance. Moreover, this chapter underscores various success stories that contradict the apprehension, ambiguity, and skepticism that those opposing Serverless tend to instigate.

References

[1] "Amazon cloud chief jabs Oracle: 'Customers are sick of it'." www.cnbc.com/2017/04/19/amazon-aws-chief-andy-jassy-on-oracle-customers-are-sick-of-it.html

[2] "Microsoft Audits." https://microsoftaudits.com/

[3] "Don't get locked up into avoiding lock-in." https://martinfowler.com/articles/oss-lockin.html

[4] Debate over Cloudinary vs. running image manipulation locally. https://news.ycombinator.com/item?id=14612332

[5] "Can I bulk download all of my Cloudinary resources?" https://support.cloudinary.com/hc/en-us/articles/203068641-Can-I-bulk-download-all-of-my-Cloudinary-resources-

[6] "Migrate sensitive payments data." https://stripe.com/docs/security/data-migrations

[7] "New - Provisioned Concurrency for Lambda Functions." https://aws.amazon.com/blogs/aws/new-provisioned-concurrency-for-lambda-functions/

[8] "What is Algolia's product compliance?" www.algolia.com/doc/faq/security-privacy/product-compliance/

[9] "Security, Privacy & Compliance." https://auth0.com/security

[10] "A guide to PCI compliance." https://stripe.com/guides/pci-compliance

[11] "Serverless IoT @iRobot." www.infoq.com/presentations/serverless-iot-irobot/

[12] https://twitter.com/ben11kehoe/status/1475556704473399297

[13] "Accelerating with Serverless!" https://medium.com/lego-engineering/accele-rating-with-serverless-625da076964b

[14] "Why Lego Went Cloud and Serverless to Handle Traffic Spikes." www.informationweek.com/cloud/why-lego-went-cloud-and-serverless-to-handle-traffic-spikes/d/d-id/1339742

[15] "How The COVID Tracking Project Scaled From 0 to 2M API Requests in 3 Months." www.netlify.com/blog/2020/07/06/how-the-covid-tracking-project-scaled-from-0-to-2m-api-requests-in-3-months/

[16] "AWS Serverless Customer Success." https://aws.amazon.com/serverless/customers

Chapter 5

Introducing Branch

Earlier chapters laid out the details and theory behind the benefits of Serverless architectures over traditional ones, but theory alone can be useless. Branch, a rapidly growing insurance company based in the United States, has been following the Serverless architecture practices described in this book. It offers a pertinent example for understanding the practical benefits of going Serverless.

Serverless from the Start

I am the chief technology officer and cofounder of Branch,[1] the only personal lines insurance company in the United States that enables the instant purchase of home and car insurance. The Serverless principles within this book were at the heart of Branch from the beginning. Before anyone at Branch wrote a single line of code, we wrote down our primary principle and corollary.

Branch Primary Development Principle

When we write code, we optimize for maintainability.

We build systems that can be maintained by the average developer, as opposed to needing ninjas, geniuses, or rockstars, who often choose to optimize for their own interests over systems that stand the test of time.

> ### Corollary
>
> The easiest systems to maintain are those that we do not build, run, or maintain, but those that we pay others to build, run, and maintain. The most maintainable code is no code.

We choose to optimize for maintainability because a core part of our strategy requires being able to develop software at a high rate of output for many years. Companies that optimize for getting a minimum viable product (MVP) out the door can quickly end up with significant technical debt and difficulties in shipping new features even a few years after the MVP. We believe that any organization that plans on building software over time and at scale will achieve more by optimizing for maintainability over other goals.

The Problem to Solve

Branch was built to solve a problem that its founders saw in personal lines insurance in the United States. Insurers spend around 25% of the money they bring in on acquiring new customers, even with economies of scale and even as the cost of paying claims has continued to rise. In this era of software, automation, the Internet, and smartphones, the potential cost of home and car insurance should have been decreasing, but it wasn't. The reason insurers continue to spend more money on acquiring customers is that insurance is difficult to buy; people find it painful to shop around. Accordingly, the first or second place someone turns for insurance often wins, even if another, lesser-known option is cheaper and better.

Branch was built to sell insurance at "insurance moments," when someone is buying or refinancing a home or a car, by leveraging its technology and insurance product expertise. By building sophisticated, modern insurance products that can be purchased in seconds with minimal data entry and then integrating them with partners who are handling the underlying home or car transaction, Branch cuts out many of the costs that are traditionally allocated to acquiring customers.

Key Differentiators/What to Build

Insurance is a complicated business that requires a significant number of processes, people, and technology to run. Every insurance company built in the United States *except for Branch* launched with a single line of insurance at its beginning because of how different the requirements are for each. To sell its first policies, Branch needed to be able to build insurance products (up to tens of thousands of pages for each product in each state, most of which are printed-out Excel tables detailing insurance pricing algorithms). It also needed to underwrite those products, handle regulatory compliance, file mandated reports, pass technical and accounting audits, and staff the phones with licensed sales and service staff—and that doesn't include any technology budget.

Using Branch's Serverless philosophy, the main question to answer was, "What is it that Branch has to build and cannot buy?" Branch started by trying not to write any custom code at all. Branch built its initial prototype with a no-code platform, Bubble.[2] Branch pushed Bubble to its limits, finding that it was possible to use a managed service, ClarionDoor,[3] for calculating rates and generating required forms. Branch also experimented with Software-as-a-Service (SaaS) offerings for insurance companies that can run all operations for more traditional insurers. Ultimately, however, Branch's plan to control the user experience at a very fine-grained level, combined with the desire to make it possible to buy home and car insurance in seconds in a single transaction, forced Branch to develop its purchase experience in-house.

In addition, Branch could not find a way to provide the user experience it wanted beyond the initial purchase for its members on the web and in mobile apps without building those itself, so they were added to the build list. But everything else could be bought, so Branch set out to do just that.

What to Buy

Branch was able to buy many pieces that other startups, founded around the same time, decided to build: an underwriting and support ticketing system (ZenDesk), omnichannel communication platforms (ZenDesk for members, Five9 for prospects), a rating engine (ClarionDoor), a forms generator (ClarionDoor), a claims management system (Snapsheet), an accounting system (QuickBooks Online), a customer data platform (Segment), a custom email campaign tool (Customer.io), and a search engine (Algolia), among others. Executives at Branch didn't necessarily see these services as perfect—or even meeting all the features that they wanted to have. But they did recognize the value of getting up and running quickly and being able to use them to understand better how and when (if ever) Branch would need to move to different systems.

Using so much SaaS at Branch has involved so many wonderful aspects. Every department has been fully in charge of the configuration and use of the software that matters the most to it. An entire book could be written about empowering departments to own their key vendor relationships, even if those vendors are SaaS vendors; that is not the focus of this book, but it is very much in alignment with the principles laid out in the Amazon memo in Chapter 3, "Serverless Architectures," and with the Serverless mindset.

To the extent that Branch has a central information technology organization, it is focused on information security and enabling Branchers to successfully use technology. Central information technology at Branch does not slow down adoption or prevent the full use of products, provided that they meet information security guidelines. Departments interact directly with the software providers, so they get direct expert advice and configuration. Additionally, many leaders in companies over the past decades have realized that they were wrong in at least some of their initial beliefs about how they would want to use the software and what their key needs would be. Instead of spending a lot of development dollars building the wrong thing, Branch has been able to use the work of other developers (and their customer success teams) to identify the best possible ways to succeed. Finally, buying over building has made it much easier for Branch to make changes when it has needed to—for example, when it switched from QuickBooks Online to NetSuite because of the increasing complexity of its accounting needs.

Minimize the Innovation Tokens

Dan McKinley, previously a principal engineer at Etsy, wrote an influential and powerful article about how to build software systems entitled "Choose Boring Technology."[4] McKinley's thesis is that it's better to work with languages, tools, frameworks, and patterns that have been tried and tested throughout the years. If an organization wants to leverage some new technologies, it should do so sparingly. McKinley calls the use of a new technology "spending innovation tokens" and says that an organization can't use many tokens before the innovation will go broke. After all, using new technologies can incur a compounding impact as an organization struggles to understand how the technologies interact with each other.

It might be surprising to find a book about embracing a different way of building software—Serverlessly—citing a philosophy around using proven technologies, but Branch has been sparing in the innovation tokens it has spent. What McKinley doesn't address in his essay is that, with so many different proven technologies today, it is very difficult to find people who have experience with all of them. Thus, there is a need to discover proven, "boring" technologies. One might read McKinley's article as a defense of "use only what *you* know," but that's not correct. You almost certainly don't know *most* of the proven technologies that you could leverage, but once you identify them, you should be able to rely upon mostly proven technologies.

In July 2019, when Branch sold its first insurance policies, almost all the managed services and SaaS it relied upon had been around for more than 5 years, and each had significant market share and marquee customers in its category. Perhaps the only innovation token Branch spent was on AWS AppSync, which Branch selected before it became generally available in April 2018. Branch chose AppSync because it dramatically reduced the number of lines of code Branch needed to write and the systems that Branch needed to run. If AppSync had not worked out, Branch would have built an AppSync replacement.

Minimize the Number of Technologies

Jonathan Murray, formerly the chief technology officer at Warner Music Group, considers the conflict inherent in needing to empower teams to build quickly while also needing to prevent the chaos that results as teams pick many different but similar technologies. Murray sees a solution to this problem in the "composable enterprise," where a team of technical leaders approve which technologies can be used and create time and space to migrate from deprecated choices to better ones chosen more recently.[5]

At Branch, we have embraced the philosophy of minimizing the number of different technologies that we use. When a service from Amazon Web Services (AWS) is at least as good as its alternatives, we use AWS. For example, we use Cognito for user authentication, even though alternatives such as Auth0 offer advantages over Cognito, because Cognito is sufficient for our use and integrates more easily with other AWS services, such as AppSync. That said, Branch will leave the AWS service for a new service if there are significant benefits to be gained, such as moving from AWS CloudFront and S3 to Vercel to host front-end applications.

Additionally, when Branch has a pattern that we know works well (for example, using AWS Simple Queue Service queues to trigger asynchronous custom code in AWS Lambda functions), we prefer to use it for cases that can use it, even if, in isolation, another pattern might seem optimal (for example, AWS Step Functions). At Branch, we spend a significant amount of time researching the best options before we build something significant, and then we build in a certain amount of inertia around those architectural choices. That inertia forces new alternatives to be obviously and significantly better. Once those alternatives are found, however, Branch seeks to move everything from the old choice to the new choice over time.

Organizational Overview

Branch is an insurance company, and the products it makes and sells are insurance products. Branch leverages technology to deliver differentiated experiences to its members and partners, so it has a modern technology organization as well. Additionally, as with all organizations of a significant size, Branch has a need for typical departments such as people operations, legal, sales, and support.

Top-Level Departments

Branch's top-level departments are titled Insurance Product, Claims, Finance, Direct Sales, Support, Agency Sales, Business Development, Legal, Operations, People Operations, and Technology. Each of these departments has a well-defined area of responsibility and a leader who works within a leadership team that meets regularly.

Technology Organization

The Branch technology organization is broken into three primary categories: technical product, design, and software development. One aspect that makes Branch's technology organization different from most other companies' is that people within each department grow to interact with all elements of Branch's technology systems. There are no hard divisions by systems; for example, there isn't a permanent "API team" that works on only APIs and doesn't touch anything else ever. No permanent "front end" team works only on front-end applications and never anything else.

Branch's technology organization runs domain-aligned teams because there is significant value in having domain-specific experience and understanding for more efficient and effective software development. Branch's Serverless architecture makes having domain-aligned teams that work cross-functionally much easier to assemble and maintain than with a traditional software development architecture.

Technical Product

At Branch, what is often just called the "product" department is the "technical product" department because the primary product Branch sells is insurance, and there is a separate (and much larger) insurance product department managing it. The technical product department at Branch is responsible for soliciting, discovering, nurturing, developing, and managing all software and systems development, from specification through going live. Product managers (PMs) at Branch get experience with all the systems at Branch. For smaller units of time, however, they tend to work on specific business objectives (such as improving online conversion) that impact a subset of systems. PMs determine what the design and development teams do on a daily and weekly basis, from the list of available items that they have cultivated.

Design

The Branch design department takes on problems identified by key stakeholders within Branch and refined through its product management team. Branch designers are responsible for applying brand and technical design guidelines to problems and determining how interfaces should be created and modified to solve those problems.

Branch designers deliver both the visual user interface and user interaction/experience designs, in high fidelity.

Software Development

Branch hires what traditionally might be called front-end developers, but because Branch's systems are Serverless and Branch uses JavaScript and TypeScript for all its code, incoming front-end developers can fairly easily learn how to build within each of Branch's projects. This model is not unique to Branch: Nader Dabit, a developer-author, has written a book entitled *Full Stack Serverless*[6] that details how to build as a full-stack developer with only front-end experience. Every developer at Branch is simply a developer who can work on all code and infrastructure at Branch.

Additionally, this strategy allows Branch to hire more junior developers than senior developers. As of late 2022, more than half of Branch's software development team had less than 2 years' experience working full time in software development; around three-quarters of the team members started their software development career at Branch.

Missing Roles

Finally, Branch does not currently employ any employees who work as systems administrators, network administrators, database administrators, systems reliability engineers (SREs), or DevOps. Branch's Serverless systems enable Branch developers to architect, build, deploy, and run everything. Other organizations need these roles because the complexity of them has been insourced to the organization. However, at Branch, traditional tasks such as systems administration and network administration do not exist—there are no servers, virtual machines, or containers to administer, as well as no networks to configure and protect. The datastores used by Branch software do not require database administration because they work directly with the code and because cloud providers take care of all scaling, backups, and restores. DevOps work is handled by development leadership because it is essentially reduced to configuring cloud services such as CircleCI and GitHub. And other than bugs introduced by custom code, service outages are handled completely by cloud providers; an SRE can do nothing to bring things back faster.

Architectural Overview and Cloud Bill

It is common to build network diagrams to depict how traditional software systems work, but the focus on the "network" makes less sense in Serverless architectures. Serverless architectures tend not to use private networks and don't have individual servers or virtual machines. As a result, it makes more sense to think about an overall architecture diagram that connects interfaces to managed services and also connects managed services to each other, with arrows depicting which system calls which.

Branch's transactional architecture is quite simple, even though it powers a full-stack insurance company. Individual front-end applications that run on clients (smartphones and web browsers) call AWS AppSync instances, which, in turn, route those requests to other managed services or custom code, based on the call (see Figure 5.1). Branch also has a back-office reporting architecture, wherein data flows from DynamoDB and other managed services to Google BigQuery, where it is mainly queried by Looker.

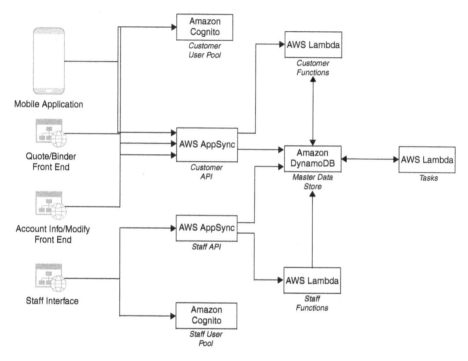

Figure 5.1 *Branch High-Level Systems Architecture*

Branch runs more than 60 Amazon accounts, each of which is a replica of production and uses the same infrastructure-as-code as the Branch production environment. This allows every developer to have an individual, isolated account and ensures that every staging and testing environment remains separate and isolated. This means that no developer or tester is ever blocking any other developer or tester, and it also makes it easy to replicate and fix issues across environments.

Branch uses many managed services beyond the infrastructure and code run at Amazon. Some of these services are insurance specific (for example, ClarionDoor for rating and generating forms), and some are high-level services for common functions (such as Stripe for billing and Algolia for searching). These services often provide separate "development" or "staging" environments, or provide ways to create a multitude of different "environments." Branch integrates its multitude of isolated Amazon account environments with these services in different ways, based on cost and effort. The most common integration is for every Branch developer and staging environment to integrate with the "development" environment for the service and for Branch production to integrate with the production environment for the service. In some instances, Branch builds out a separate "environment" to match each "environment" within Branch (for example, putting the environment name in index names in Algolia).

Cloud Bills

One significant benefit to Serverless architectures is that they do not require paying for computer hardware that is not in use; every billed cent on a cloud bill relates to a request for a system doing work. Two corresponding downsides affect cloud billing with Serverless architectures: Increased usage results in increased bills, so if one does not plan perfectly, billing will be hard to predict. Additionally, in some cases, paying on demand can end up being more expensive than paying for reserved capacity for consistent loads. Neither of these downsides tends to lead to overall more expensive bills in Serverless than traditionally architected systems.

Figure 5.2 shows Branch's cloud spend across all Amazon accounts (including all development, staging, and testing environments) from August 2020 through July 2021.

The total cost during this period increased from $1,019.24 to $3,496.65, primarily driven by DynamoDB ($400.88 to $1,872.41). The cost of running Branch back-end custom code, through Lambda, reached a mere $232.69 by July 2021. At peak loads over this time period, Branch handled more than 100 requests per second and generated more than 1,000,000 insurance offers per month. Branch continues to grow, and so does its Amazon bill, although at a rate less than Branch's top-line revenue is increasing.

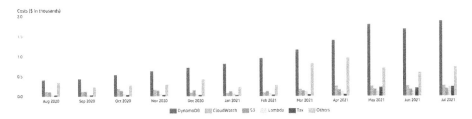

Figure 5.2 *Branch Amazon Cloud Costs*

It is worth noting that Branch spends significantly more on managed services than it does on its Amazon bill. The difficulty in making an apples-to-apples comparison on a cloud bill perspective to another company is that Branch spends less in software development expense when leveraging managed services because it is leveraging the development effort of the managed-service provider. In the end, the best comparison to be made is a combination of what a company spends on all technology and development costs versus other companies' similar expenditures.

The Branch Software Development Lifecycle

Running an effective software development lifecycle (SDLC) is critical to any company's success in developing, deploying, and running software. Branch is no exception. This section summarizes how Branch runs its SDLC to maximize its overall bandwidth of high-quality software development that is responsive to business needs.

Problem Definition

The first step in the Branch SDLC is problem definition. Requests for software development come from many sources—department heads, customers, employees, insurance product, technical product, and so on—and all of them are refined and explored into a problem. Every requested piece of development should solve a problem, and validating that the development is complete should at least partly consist of verifying that the problem is now solved. The technical product team oversees the task of ensuring that the problem is well defined and properly documented.

If the problem is complex enough, the technical product team sometimes runs a kickoff meeting in which the problem is discussed with all stakeholders who care about the problem, along with the technical product, design, and development team members who will work on the problem. In this meeting, all participants have the opportunity to ask questions to better understand the problem, and everyone can suggest different solutions and interface designs (sometimes by having a sketching period in which everyone draws with sharpies on blank paper). This brings critical information and understanding to the very beginning of the development process, which makes the designs and development more responsive and drives greater satisfaction and trust in the final product.

Design

After defining the problem, one or more members of the design department work on creating user interface and user experience designs. For large projects, this sometimes starts with lower-fidelity designs; ultimately, the designers will produce high-fidelity, to-the-pixel designs. These designs can be accepted by the relevant stakeholders, in which case they move on to development. However, the stakeholders can also reject the designs with comments, and then the designers use those comments to redesign. Accordingly, there is no fixed expectation on how long a particular problem will spend in design. The larger the problem is to be solved, the larger the set of designs is and, as expected, the more revisions tend to be needed. Additionally, some problems do not require any visual or user experience design, so they skip the design process entirely once they have been properly defined.

Software Product

After designs have been accepted, the software product team helps prioritize and schedule development. The technical product team runs refinement meetings each week to make sure that developers have everything they need to do the development. Branch uses a Kanban-style board to list development items that are ready to be worked, and developers select from those boards when they are ready to take on their issue.

Development

In most cases, developers can work on issues to initial completion without asking questions of design or stakeholders or other technical team members. Additionally, because they work in completely isolated AWS accounts, they cannot be blocked by another developer or tester who breaks something. When developers complete their work, they open a pull request in GitHub, which must pass automated tests run by CircleCI and also pass code review by one or more members of the development team.

On Trunk-Based Development and Pull Requests

The development team at Branch finds the pull request functionality within GitHub to be exceptionally useful in onboarding and training new developers, especially junior developers. The ability to run automated tests and block merges until reviews and tests are passing is a critical part of code quality processes at Branch. That said, developers at Branch try to have short-lived branches and generally like the idea of getting as close to trunk-based development as possible while still leveraging the benefits of pull requests.

Deployment

When all tests and code review(s) pass, the code is merged into the trunk branch of the code repository. At least once per day, an automated test suite runs end-to-end tests across all systems. If the tests pass, a production release deploys. If Branch sees elevated error rates in response to the release, it is easy to manually deploy an older release (or to quickly patch, if that is simpler).

Branch has not implemented any automated rollback functionality because the robustness of Branch's automated testing limits most bugs to edge-case scenarios. Thus, bugs are usually detected several releases after they were introduced, so rolling back one release would not eliminate the bug. Rolling several releases backward usually creates more pain for users than the edge-case bug that has been found. Cherry-picking the flawed code often creates merge-conflict pain. Thus, it is often much easier and faster to fix the bug quickly and roll forward.

Infrastructure

All Branch infrastructure exists as code (YAML) executed through the AWS Serverless Application Model (SAM) client. SAM is essentially a superset of CloudFormation that runs CloudFormation under the hood. To manage the deployment of infrastructure across its many different AWS accounts, Branch runs Doppler,[7] which manages the different environmental variables necessary for each individual environment.

Running

All errors in production come in two varieties: bugs in Branch's code and incidents with managed services. The vendors themselves fix the latter issues. During the past two years, most production issues have been intermittent slowdowns in data vendor APIs that Branch relies upon to price its insurance products. Branch's yearly total downtime has ranged between a low of 28 minutes and a high of 9 hours for each year it has been in business.

Branch's operational response process has evolved throughout the years to have two separate paths: (1) Where a particular type of error is known to be connected to a managed service, the staff using that service contact the service directly. (2) Everything else goes to the on-call Branch senior development leaders.

For example, if phone calls are not being routed properly to support staff, the on-call support staff leadership knows how to escalate to the telephony vendor. If insurance rates are not being returned properly from the insurance rating managed service, Branch's internal application prints information about the degraded performance, and leaders know how to escalate with that vendor.

In contrast, if the issue is not immediately connectable to a vendor, Branch's internal teams escalate to the on-call Branch development team, which consists of rotating senior developers. Those developers investigate the issue and identify whether it is the result of a bug in Branch code or whether it is a managed service; then the developers escalate accordingly. Another benefit of every Branch developer being able to work on every part of Branch's codebase is that the senior developers on call are usually able to identify problems themselves, without further escalation.

Summary: Branch

Earlier chapters laid out the details and theory behind the benefits of Serverless architectures over traditional ones, but theory in isolation can be useless. Branch, a rapidly growing insurance company based in the United States, has been following the Serverless architecture practices described in this book and is a prime example to illustrate the benefits of going Serverless.

Branch builds systems that can be maintained by the average developer. We chose to optimize for maintainability because a core part of our strategy requires being able to develop software at a high rate of output for many years.

Branch's software architecture allows it to run small, cross-functional teams to build software. Therefore, Branch does not need many roles that exist in organizations that do not build Serverlessly. Branch's spend on primary cloud services is very low relative to the equivalent non-Serverless expenditure. Finally, the chapter concludes with details on how Branch tactically handles software development with its Serverless architecture.

References

[1] Branch. www.branch.com/

[2] Bubble. https://bubble.io/

[3] ClarionDoor, www.clariondoor.com/

[4] "Choose Boring Technology." https://mcfunley.com/choose-boring-technology

[5] "The Composable Enterprise." www.adamalthus.com/blog/2013/04/04/the-composable-enterprise/

[6] Dabit, Nader. *Full Stack Serverless: Modern Application Development with React, AWS, and Graphql.* O'Reilly Media, 2020.

[7] Doppler. www.doppler.com/

Chapter 6

Introducing Insureco

To evaluate the business benefits of Serverless over more traditional software architectures, we need a stalking horse comparison to Branch, the Serverless insurance company introduced in the previous chapter. Insureco, a hypothetical insurance company that has undergone a complete digital transformation, serves as that foil. In this chapter, Insureco comes to life with details derived from recent best-practices articles, to set up Chapter 7, "The Clash of Cultures," as a comparison between Branch and Insureco.

The History of Insureco

Insureco was founded as part of a department store in the 1950s, to take advantage of the low cost of acquiring the store's existing automotive supply and repair customers for a new auto insurance product. Insureco was able to offer a cheaper price for many customers and subsequently added on a homeowner's insurance product, which it could also offer at a justifiably lower price.

Originally, Insureco operated all its business on paper: Customers filled out a single-page insurance application and wrote a check. The application was reviewed the following week, the check was cashed, and if everything was in order, a clerk filled out insurance cards and mailed them to the customer. The pricing algorithm for insurance was simple: It just required looking up a few values in a three-ring binder and then doing simple arithmetic with them. Even when Insureco started selling through independent agents, it was able to keep things on paper for quite a long time.

Over time, however, as Insureco got bigger, customers wanted easier and faster processing of their insurance applications. Additionally, the pricing algorithms got more complicated, which increased the likelihood of error when looking up values in the binder and doing increasingly complicated math. Customers also expected faster resolution of their insurance claims. All of this led Insureco to adopt different technology solutions over the following decades, starting with mainframes and eventually moving to offering 24×7 purchasing online powered by a public cloud provider. The company even developed a mobile app to handle everything that customers are allowed to self-serve.

Organizational Structure

Insureco has a typical enterprise organizational chart (see Figure 6.1), separating what it calls the "what" from the "how" of development. The marketing department owns the customer experience both pre- and post-sale; marketing is tasked with both identifying and converting prospects, and it is also responsible for the net promoter score of its existing customers. The chief information officer oversees the implementation of everything that Insureco calls "technology" or "digital," from making sure that employees are equipped with the right hardware and Internet access to work from home, to building and running all the custom software that Insureco creates.

Key Performance Indicators

At Insureco, the primary key performance indicator is the growth of insurance premiums. Every year, Insureco wants to see the total amount of insurance premiums it charges increase by at least 2%. Almost as important is hitting its expense targets, especially around sales and marketing spend, but also on its digital and innovation projects.

Insureco next watches its competitive positioning and its customer satisfaction ratings because the company has not been growing its customer base. In fact, its compound annual growth rate (CAGR) of revenue has stayed in the 2% range, even though the cost of insurance has been increasing at an average of 5% per year. This is because Insureco consistently loses more customers every year than it gains. Insureco believes that the only way to reverse these trends is to use technology to bring better experiences and lower prices to customers, which is why it is so invested in its digital capabilities.

Digital Transformation

Recently, Insureco completed several key steps in its digital transformation plan, which it has been working on since 2017.[1] Insureco has hired new technology staff and retrained existing staff to be able to empower smaller teams to ship new software every 2 weeks. It is now running nearly all its infrastructure on Kubernetes,

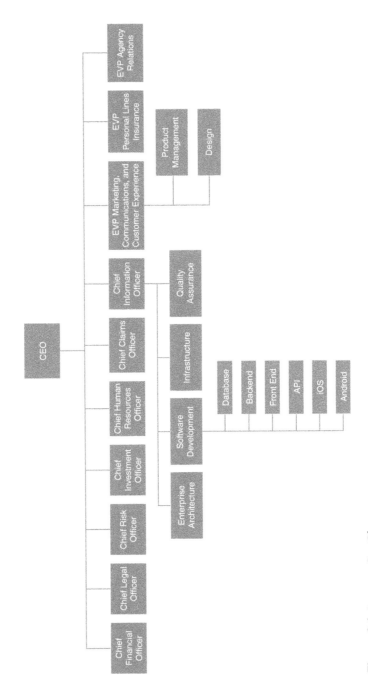

Figure 6.1 *Insureco Org Chart*

which has required a separate team of Kubernetes experts and systems reliability engineers (SREs). However, its teams are now able to deploy and roll back with only quality assurance team sign-off instead of requiring infrastructure team members to schedule and individually release.

Marketing Organization

Insureco's marketing division oversees all customer experience and drives customers into its sales funnel. This allows Insureco to centralize its design and UX employees and decisions.

Project/Product Management

Insureco has both project and product managers to handle all its marketing campaigns, design projects, and software development specifications. Insureco's product managers are professionally trained software product managers who understand agile software development and know how to write software specifications. They oversee building personas, developing and testing hypotheses for future software development projects, running usability tests, and defining all the "what" that is built by Insureco's tech teams.

Design

Insureco's design team does visual design, graphic design, product marketing design, and all the software designs (web, mobile web, and mobile apps). Designers work closely with product managers to build prototypes that are tested with real users and then build the final pixel-perfect designs that go to the software developers.

Technology Organization

Insureco's technology organization develops, builds, tests, and runs all the software with which Insureco prospects and customers interact. Insureco's technology leadership delegates to the marketing organization the "what" that is built and focuses entirely on "how" the software is built. This division of responsibility is necessary because of the large number of choices that need to be made about how to develop, build, test, and run software at Insureco. The complexity is evident from the large number of divisions within the technology organization.

Enterprise Architecture

Enterprise architects (EAs) at Insureco ensure that developers at Insureco are not making unreliable, insecure, or unnecessarily complex choices when they decide how to build software. EAs create all software development specifications that involve greenfield software projects or the adoption of new technology that is not currently in the allowed set of building blocks in the composable enterprise (see Chapter 5, "Introducing Branch," and the relevant reference for an explanation). Enterprise architects are also responsible for selecting which technologies to add and remove from the allowed set.[2]

Software Development

The software development division at Insureco is divided into many teams, each of which has a specialized knowledge of a particular category of technologies. This specialization is necessary because each of the technologies is quite complicated and requires significant expertise to build software to required specifications that interacts appropriately with all the other teams' creations.

Insureco software developers are interested in microservices architectures, running containers on Kubernetes and polyglot programming. They like to try new technologies they read about and underestimate the risk these new technologies introduce to the organization.[3]

Database

The database team at Insureco handles multiple types of databases that are used by Insureco's software products. Insureco has finally completed migration of all the software that uses relational databases to SQL Server, which has reduced what Insureco has to support. Despite that, Insureco still has a full team of SQL Server experts who are needed to ensure that database designs are done in proper third-normal form with the right indexes and foreign keys; to make sure that stored procedures, triggers, and views are set up correctly; and to verify that database servers are appropriately tuned as workloads grow and change. Additionally, Insureco has experts in Redis, Elasticsearch, Kafka, Cassandra, and AWS Redshift because of the different needs of the different applications Insureco builds and runs.

Front End

The front-end development team at Insureco builds all the websites—for desktop, tablet, and mobile users—that Insureco needs to sell and support its insurance products. The team uses React as its primary framework but also runs a number of WordPress sites so that the marketing team can update content in systems that it can manage.

Back End

The back-end development team at Insureco is responsible for all the business logic needed for Insureco's operations: quoting insurance, purchasing insurance, generating documents (including ID cards), changing payment information, changing insurance policy details (such as adding cars, adding drivers, and changing mortgage lenders), billing, cancelling policies for various reasons, and generating data for reporting. The back-end team uses C# and the .NET framework, along with the Business Rules Framework, to build out all its business logic.

API

The API team at Insureco is responsible for connecting the front-end applications (built by the front-end team and the mobile teams) to the back-end teams' business logic, as well as allowing APIs for third parties outside Insureco to make authorized calls into Insureco's systems. The API team uses ASP.NET and Power Apps as its primary tools.

iOS/Android

Insureco writes code natively for both iOS and Android. This requires separate teams because it is difficult to find developers who specialize in both mobile operating systems. The teams work from similar specifications but deviate in implementation where interface/interactions conventions and underlying libraries differ. The separate teams also allow Insureco to focus on the increasingly divergent privacy rules and permission notifications for each ecosystem and app store.

Infrastructure

To support the underlying software development processes and running software at Insureco, the Infrastructure division has separate teams for CI/CD, Kubernetes, and Site Reliability Engineering (SRE).[4]

Quality Assurance

Last but not least, QA is run by the software development organization, handling functional, acceptance, and security testing. The QA team creates and maintains automated tests that are integrated in CI/CD pipelines, as well as manual tests that are not possible to automate effectively.

Architectural Overview

Insureco runs its internal CI/CD pipelines as well as its production infrastructure on Kubernetes on Azure (see Figure 6.2). Its embrace of Site Reliability Engineering has allowed its infrastructure team to provide common interfaces and rules to developers so that all infrastructure is containerized in ways that are possible for it to maintain centrally.[5]

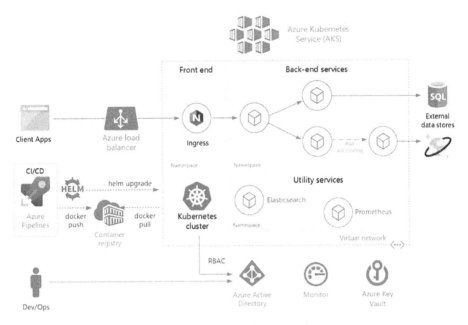

Figure 6.2 *Microsoft Azure Well-Architected Reference Architecture*

The Insureco Software Development Lifecycle

The Insureco SDLC runs in 2-week sprints. Before each sprint begins, product managers meet with software development team leads and enterprise architects to verify that an appropriate amount of work is being allocated to a sprint and that designs are ready to go. Sprints usually kick off on a Thursday, development runs through the following Friday, and fixes in response to QA are done the next Monday through Wednesday, with a release targeted for Wednesday at noon.

UI/UX Design

The design team builds most of its designs in advance of work assignment to a sprint. Designers seek to build pixel-perfect designs for different screen sizes, along with interaction mockups so that animations and transition specifications are easy to understand. Once the work is assigned within a sprint, the design team is available for adjustments and for answering questions.

Product

The product management team runs the sprint process, with both product managers and scrum masters scheduling meetings and assigning work to developers and QA team members. In general, product managers work with the same sets of developers from sprint to sprint, although realignments do happen, based on turnover or the difficulty or importance of various projects.

Developers

Front-end, back-end, mobile, and API developers often work together in Spotify-like "squad" scrum teams.[6] This enables them to build features and functionality that come completely from the product and design teams, without depending on other scrum teams for release, except for integration testing. Engineering managers in each of the individual teams can be called on for code review or other skill-based mentoring of individual developers within scrum teams. Occasionally, a scrum team consists only of members of a single development discipline, such as for a new public-facing API, where only API developers might be working, or for a new marketing website, where only front-end developers might be involved.

Infrastructure

The infrastructure teams at Insureco set forth all the rules and guides that developers need to follow to develop, build, test, and run the software that they build. Team members are available to assist developers in following those rules and guides during sprints, and they also respond to asynchronous alerts from monitoring systems that they have set up.

Deploying

When QA has approved the release of new code from a sprint, the infrastructure team is notified that the release is ready to go live in production. For the infrastructure team to support and own the running production infrastructure, the infrastructure team decides when to do the actual release to the production infrastructure and then monitors errors to see if a rollback is required. For most products, the infrastructure team uses a blue/green deployment strategy with canaries that gradually shifts traffic to the newly released code; it reverses that traffic allocation only if it sees a significant new set of errors coming from the new release.

Running

With the SRE model, most of the responsibility for ensuring that the Insureco infrastructure stays online rests with the infrastructure team members. Their collection of monitored metrics syndicated through their paging system helps identify most issues early, and they have developed runbooks for their on-call staff to remediate most issues whenever they begin to show up. If an error reported to the infrastructure team is specific to custom code from a developer, that error is referred to the business unit that owns that product to decide whether (a) the bug should be fixed and a hotfix patch released, (b) the bug should be fixed in the next sprint release, and/or (c) the SRE team should roll back to the previous release.

Life at Insureco

By modern best practices, as detailed in the "References" section for this chapter, Insureco is doing as much right as can be expected. Most other companies would like to be as organized as Insureco in how it develops, builds, deploys, and runs its software. However, as the next chapter points out, Insureco is at a significant disadvantage in how quickly and effectively it can build software.

Summary: Insureco

This chapter offers an organizational example to match the theoretical explanations of the benefits of Serverless architectures, introducing Insureco, a software development "best practices" (but not Serverless) organization.

Insureco is designed to be an example of what traditional software architects tend to recommend: scrum teams building with containers and using reference architectures from cloud providers. Insureco also uses some oft-copied organizational ideas taken from both Spotify and Google. Insureco's practices should seem very familiar to most technology professionals.

References

[1] "Digitalization Strategy for Business Transformation," Gartner. https://www.gartner.com/en/information-technology/insights/digitalization

[2] The term *composable enterprise* was coined by Jonathan in 2013 (www.adamalthus.com/blog/2013/04/04/the-composable-enterprise/) but has been misattributed to Gartner, who used the term and context without attribution (https://www.gartner.com/en/doc/465932-future-of-applications-delivering-the-composable-enterprise).

[3] "Microservices architecture on Azure Kubernetes Service." https://learn.microsoft.com/en-us/azure/architecture/reference-architectures/containers/aks-microservices/aks-microservices

[4] "What is Site Reliability Engineering (SRE)?" https://sre.google/

[5] "A Reference Implementation Demonstrating Microservices Architecture and Best Practices for Microsoft Azure." https://github.com/mspnp/microservices-reference-implementation

[6] "Scaling Agile @ Spotify with Tribes, Squads, Chapters & Guilds." https://blog.crisp.se/wp-content/uploads/2012/11/SpotifyScaling.pdf

Chapter 7

The Clash of Cultures

Using the example companies of Branch (see Chapter 5, "Introducing Branch") and Insureco (see Chapter 6, "Introducing Insureco,"), this chapter compares the capability of each business to achieve business outcomes as a direct capability stemming from its software, business, and social architectures and its associated organizational structure. The point of this chapter is not to make an argument that all "Insurecos" will operate as the median-case Insureco details here; instead, this chapter illustrates how much easier it is to succeed with Branch's architectures than with a traditional architecture. Branch leverages what Serverless enables in technological, social, and business organization to drive superior results.

The Drivers of the Business Benefits of Technology

In 1997, Paul Strassman, formerly the CIO at Xerox, published *The Squandered Computer*, a book with comprehensive evidence that increased spending on technology does not guarantee better business outcomes. Strassman recognized that technology and computers are critical to business operations but identified that organizations could not spend their way to success.[1] This is just as true today as it was 25 years ago: Immense benefits can be farmed from the adoption of technology, but simply spending money on it is insufficient to drive those results.

If spend alone cannot dictate success, what is a better measure of whether organizations can pull more value out of the technology they adopt? Simon Wardley, a well-known proponent of cloud computing and the inventor of Wardley Mapping, outlines this another way: maximizing componentization.[2] Applying Herbert Simon's theory of hierarchy, Wardley explains:

Simon Wardley on Componentization

In the Theory of Hierarchy,[3] Herbert Simon showed how the creation of a system is dependent upon the organisation of its subsystems. As an activity becomes commoditised and provided as ever more standardised components, it not only allows for increasing speed of implementation, but also rapid change, diversity, and agility of systems that are built upon it.

In other words, it's faster to build a house with commodity components such as bricks, wooden planks, and plastic pipes than it is to start from first principles with a clay pit, a clump of trees, and an oil well.

Bricks, planks, and pipes along with other architectural building blocks have led to a faster rate of house building and a wider diversity of housing shapes. This is the same with electronics and every other field you care to look at. Commoditisation to standard components leads to increased agility, diversity, and speed of creation for higher order systems that are built with it.

This doesn't mean that change stops with the standard components. Take, for example, brick making or electricity provision or the manufacture of windows; there is a still significant amount of improvement hidden behind the "standard."

However, the "standard" acts as an abstraction layer to this. Just because my electricity supplier has introduced new sources of power generation (wind turbine, geothermal, etc.) doesn't mean I wake up one morning to find that we're moving from 240V 50Hz to something else.

If that constant operational improvement in electricity generation was not abstracted behind the standard, then all the consumer electronics built upon this would need to continuously change—the entire system would either collapse in a mess or, at the very least, technological progress would be hampered.

Now, as an activity evolves to a more standard, good enough commodity, then to a consumer, all this improvement is normally hidden behind the interface. Any changes are ultimately reflected in a better price or quality of service, but the activity itself, for all sense of purpose, will remain as is (e.g., a standard but cheaper brick or power supply or wooden plank).

There are exceptions to this, but it usually involves significant upheaval due to all the higher order systems that need to change, and hence government involvement is usually required (e.g., changing electricity standards, decimalisation, and the changing of currency or even simply switching from analogue to digital transmission of TV).

Hence, activities evolve to more of a commodity (i.e., linear) and those that become components act as an interface boundary between the higher order systems that consume them and operational improvement to the activity.

Thus, according to this framework, organizations that use higher-level, more abstracted components will be able to move more quickly and deliver more meaningful business results. As explained in earlier chapters of this book, Serverless architectures are exactly those higher-level components available to technologists within organizations. For example, consider four different implementations of building full-text search capabilities into an application: (1) using only code that is written by developers in the organization and that is running on containers in the cloud, (2) using some existing full-text search code (such as Lucene) and running on containers in the cloud, (3) using existing full-text search software (such as Elastic-Search) and running on containers in the cloud, or (4) using a managed service (such as Algolia) that runs itself. Moving from 1 to 4 is the process of moving from low-level components to high-level, abstracted components—and also moving from cloud to Serverless in both architecture and mindset.

Instead of having to interact with virtual servers or containers as relatively "dumb" units of compute or running various server applications and managing their interactions with custom code, Serverless takes code and configuration directly. Serverless architectures transfer lower-level management concerns to vendors and keep only the business-logic layer. Organizations that have to worry about only the business logic layer move faster than those that must be excellent at lower-level operations as well.

The rest of this chapter walks through a more detailed, nose-to-the-ground explanation of why a company such as Branch delivers significantly better business outcomes than a company such as Insureco. The chapter accomplishes its explanation in two ways. First, it discusses the specific tasks that insurance companies need to do, to explain why Branch executes better than Insureco. Second, the chapter ends with a more conceptual and general discussion of how business leaders are dissatisfied with the outcomes of their technology organizations, how they describe that dissatisfaction, and how Serverless architectures enable a paradigm shift in overall organizational satisfaction.

How U.S. Insurance Companies Drive Better Outcomes

Launch New Products, New States

Personal lines insurance companies in the United States, such as Branch and Insureco, usually grow their businesses by selling more insurance products (for example, a company that previously sold only home insurance adds car insurance to its offerings) and by selling those products in more states. In the United States, each state has its own laws and requires separate approval to sell insurance products to its citizens.

Each state can require insurers to do things differently, so an insurer's capability to grow its business is directly impacted by how quickly it can make changes in response to requirements by customers and state regulators.

Example: Uninsured Motorist Coverage

A great example of how offerings differ in each state relates to uninsured motorist coverage. Although having car insurance is a requirement to drive in every state in the United States, a significant number of people do not have car insurance. If you are hit by one of these drivers, your basic car insurance will not cover injuries to you or damage to your vehicle. This is where uninsured (or underinsured) motorist coverage comes in.

In very few cases do two states have exactly the same rules governing how insurers must offer this coverage. Some allow uninsured and underinsured coverage to be combined and to be purchased at any amount, up to the main coverage customers have purchased (if they hit someone else). Others require customers to buy uninsured and underinsured coverages separately. Others require customers to buy uninsured coverage only equal to the main coverage. Still others require insurers to offer "stacking" uninsured coverage so that you can multiply your coverage by the number of cars you have.

States also change requirements related to how insurers must offer uninsured motorist coverage. These changes are never retroactive, so insurers must support multiple regulatory requirements at once: one set for each start date of regulations. Once an insurer sells a policy, for the length of the term of that policy (usually 6 or 12 months), the insurer must be able to modify that policy and keep static the rules that were in place at the beginning of the policy static, while putting in place new rules for policies written afterward.

Insurance companies launch new states and products in this way: An insurance product team develops insurance products for particular states, submits them to states for approval, and then modifies them in response to requirements from state regulators. The insurance products themselves consist of rates (the formula that describes exactly how much the insurance will cost—essentially, an Excel spreadsheet with many inputs and a price as an output), rules (explanations of how the inputs to the rates will be determined), and forms (the actual legal contracts that govern what losses will be covered). When the rates, rules, and forms are approved by a state, they then need to be implemented so that the sales and service teams can sell and support insurance policies. The entire process of building and launching insurance products is dynamic—the insurance product team and the state can make changes from the original design—and there are significant consequences to not following the approved products exactly.

Thus, the key skills that technology teams (especially software development teams) need to have to enable a U.S. insurance company to deliver new products quickly are (a) being able to follow precise specifications and (b) being able to handle changes to those specifications after they have already begun implementation. Honing these skills enables Branch to treat new products and new states much like a change in an existing product in an existing state.

In contrast, Insureco has a much harder time making changes "in flight." The 2-week sprint at Insureco compared to the daily releases at Branch is a significant part of this difference. Branch can release an order of magnitude more times and thus learn and cycle much faster. This difference in release schedule is also the source of more reasons why Insureco is unable to adjust quickly. Stakeholders at Insureco know that they can receive new functionality only 26 times per year and that, after a desired feature is released, they have to wait at least a few cycles before the next release on their feature goes out. Therefore, they will expand their initial requests.

In other words, organizations will increase scope for requests when releases are less frequent, which will result in even longer lead times. The vicious cycle of infrequent releases leads to more infrequent new feature releases; the virtuous cycle of frequent releases leads to even more frequent new feature releases. This leads Insureco's product managers to not even try to begin work before state approval because the cost of change will often make the project take longer than simply running a pure waterfall process. Thus, what ends up happening is not "agile," but is closer to waterfall, but delivered in 2-week sprints, with some minor changes made along the way.

Improve User Experience

Purchasing and working with insurance can be a painful and slow experience, and insurers have been trying to make insurance activities easier and more self-service ever since building their first websites. Enabling customers to purchase insurance more easily leads to more customers purchasing ("converting"), which allows insurers to spend less money per policy on acquisition. Enabling customers to self-serve various policy changes yields higher customer satisfaction and reduces service costs for insurers.

Insureco can design and deploy user experience improvements, but at a slower cadence and also on a smaller scale than Branch. For Insureco to design, build, and deploy improvements, many technical teams need to understand what's needed and schedule their work and deployments. Additionally, because Insureco releases only every 2 weeks, a significant amount of time is devoted to scheduling and communicating schedules. These factors decrease the speed at which Insureco can build and release, and they also decrease the scope of what can be done. As projects get large enough to cross multiple areas of the application, change becomes so expensive (in both actual cost and opportunity cost) that it has to be a CEO-level priority to get done.

Speed of Information to Action

In general, the capability of a business to grow successfully is directly related to its ability to run quick feedback cycles: form a hypothesis, build and deploy to test the hypothesis, gather feedback from the market, and repeat. Using the language of the customer development process,[4] this becomes: discover (understand needs), validate (through a prototype), create (the actual product), and build/scale (repeating these steps continuously as the company grows). Companies that can execute these cycles quickly, with multiple cycles in parallel, should generally succeed at higher rates than those that execute them more slowly.

The key difference between Branch, running on Serverless architectures and needing less specialization, and Insureco, running on traditional architectures with more specialization, is that Branch runs cycles more quickly and can run more cycles in parallel with comparable staff than Insureco. This is largely because Branch needs talent and expertise in many fewer disciplines in order to execute. In addition, the multiple disciplines within Insureco are inherently interconnected in ways that slow down Insureco. Even if Insureco is fine with the additional cost to run operations internally, running operations internally is less efficient for Insureco to ship software more frequently.

When Insureco runs operations internally, it does not provide an interface to its operations like a managed-service provider. Managed-service providers have excellent documentation, APIs built with significant resilience, and dedicated customer support and customer success teams to help development teams launch and run their services. Internal operations teams, in contrast, rarely have any documentation, have APIs that are less robust than vendor APIs, and do not have internal success personnel to help other departments use the internal operations. Instead, many of the communications and interactions with operations teams are done on a person-to-person basis and are not automated. This is exactly the slowness and inefficiency that Jeff Bezos observed in the memo featured in Chapter 3, "Serverless Architectures," that drove him to force Amazon departments to become services.

In theory, every organization could copy the Amazon service model; in practice, almost no organizations run this way. Thus, Insureco's choices of needing to run operations, have expertise, and employ people in disciplines that are unnecessary for it to do (but that it chooses to do anyway) all actively prevent it from iterating as quickly as its potential.

How Serverless Drives Faster, Better Action

Serverless architectures are mainly relevant to software development departments because software development is such a key driver of business success. Software development also often becomes central to an organization's ability to execute. Serverless architectures can completely change how an organization thinks about building software and how effectively the organization is able to deliver business results through software.

At Insureco, most business leaders are somewhat dissatisfied with how software development happens. Most of their complaints focus on software development velocity: Business leaders at Insureco think that it takes more time than necessary to get anything developed, and large projects seem nearly impossible to get done. This leads to a software development organization that is trying to increase velocity (usually by hiring more developers) but is also held responsible for a high level of quality. An increase in velocity when a project is already under duress and stretched to deliver value generally leads to dropping quality practices, such as creating and updating automated testing. Additionally, increasing the velocity of a pipeline in which between 5 and 15 functional teams have to be involved for every single new feature is extremely difficult and quickly reaches diminishing returns.

Serverless solves this velocity problem by reducing the number of teams and people that are necessary in building and releasing new features, as well as philosophically changing what is developed internally versus what is purchased from vendors. Reducing the scope of what an organization needs to build also decreases the time to build and release new features. Additionally, Serverless makes it much easier to have every developer act as a full-stack developer, which reduces specialization and increases resiliency. This allows Branch, as opposed to Insureco, to develop less software (because more is bought), develop small-scoped software (because it is quick and fast to make changes), and put (almost) any developer on any project. All of that leads to much faster delivery of business results.

For example, Branch implements its full-text search with Algolia, a managed service that took about a week to set up and configure; during this time, developers could accomplish all the necessary work without other dependencies. In contrast, Insureco implements with ElasticSearch, which took several weeks with operations to get ElasticSearch containers up and running, and then required several more weeks with development to set up and connect ElasticSearch to code, and then finally required several more weeks with operations to get it launched into production. The business value in both cases is the same; Branch delivered it in a fraction of the time.

Most Organizations View Software Development as Too Slow

Recently, an experienced vice president of engineering on a CTO mailing list asked a common question that many technology organizations ask themselves:

Can Software Development Ever Meet Expectations?

I've been managing engineering projects for a long time. I have managed engineering teams at five different companies with very different cultures, and the one common thread is that the business always felt like engineering was moving too slowly in delivering new features and products. And simultaneously, the engineering team always felt like they were working at an unsustainable pace and that we were going to burn people out. I think the root problem is that these teams are creating completely new things (not, for example, building houses), so there is never an objective standard for what the speed should be for new products or major new features (Agile velocity measurement notwithstanding). And even the concept of speed is nebulous because schedule is only one piece of the classic triangle, along with cost and features.

So… does anyone feel like they've figured out how to answer the question of what a high-performing product development engineering team looks like? Particularly such that all the major stakeholders in a company agree that delivery speed is sufficient (or more)? And that maintains a sustainable and healthy pace for the engineers?

At Branch, business stakeholders feel that development doesn't prevent them from going as fast as they can, and developers feel that their pace is sustainable. Branch has made key choices in its Serverless mindset (not all of which are necessarily Serverless architectural choices) that make this outcome possible.

The first key choice Branch has made is that Branch buys over building whenever possible. At Branch, code is a liability, not an asset; developers seek to write, maintain, and run as little as possible. Additionally, developers optimize for maintainability so that the average developer can work with all of Branch's code. The Serverless architecture that is all in JavaScript (and TypeScript) allows every developer to be a full stack developer and ensures that much of the code can be high level and small in terms of conceptual scope. It's possible for non-Serverless organizations to make the same stack choices here, but they rarely do; most back-end-only teams choose Ruby, Python, Java, C#, or another non-JavaScript/TypeScript language. This is another example of how fragmenting the development process leads to suboptimizing organizational choices.

The second key choice Branch makes is that there is no centralized management of software, technical services, or SaaS. This means that the Branch call center software and phone system is owned by the manager of the call center team. That manager owns all the relationships and manages the employees and vendors who set it up, maintain it, and keep it running. The technology organization does centrally manage third-party risk with reviews and audits (such as SOC2), but it does not control the day-to-day management of such software. This removes one of the main unnecessary dependencies that exists at Insureco, in which the technology department seeks to have all tech relationships, decisions, management, and uptime go through the "tech" department.

The third key choice Branch makes is having a company norm related to downscoping requests for work. Branch has cultural "roots," and one is, "This is v1" (the first version). At Branch, executives constantly hold each other to defining the v1 of what's wanted because everyone recognizes that they will inevitably learn things from the initial release that will change the course of the specifications versus what an up-front waterfall spec would have defined. This would not be a possible norm if initial releases took months (or years) from initial request to deployment. But in an organization where a departmental high priority goes from initial request to v1 deployment within a week or two, the organization is fine with an iterative development approach.

These three choices give Branch two enormous advantages over Insureco. Branch avoids doing a lot of the work that is done at Insureco, in terms of both not doing some development and doing smaller-scoped development projects. Additionally, work at Branch can be maximized to the highest priority more easily because developers at Branch are more interchangeable; when every developer can do every task, everyone can be working on high-priority items.

The Importance of Organizational Attitude

Within its culture, Branch has two critical organizational attitudes that differ from Insureco's and are necessary for its success in driving better business results. First, unlike at Insureco, the Branch software developers have a strong organizational alignment and a desire to further the business's goals over their own. Second, Branch executives are expected to be capable of directly managing SaaS vendors and systems integrators. This second point is quite important: The overall strategy at Branch follows the Amazon philosophy articulated in Chapter 3, where velocity and business outcomes are tied directly to smaller, autonomous teams. Without these attitudes—specifically, without these attitudes being enforced from the very top down—it would not be possible for Branch to be as successful with its Serverless architectures as it is.

At Insureco, with its front end, back end, infrastructure, and other specializations, developers align with the specifics of their role and tend to have less complimentary views of other roles. To some extent, this is a version of the Oracle DBA problem: If an organization hires someone as an "Oracle DBA," that organization is unlikely to ever leave Oracle databases until that position is eliminated because it creates an entrenched alignment with a specific technology. In contrast, at Branch, where developers are all simply "developers," their identities are tied not to a specific technology or even specific solutions, but rather to some kind of technical work done to get software working for the organization. If no back-end work is needed for a feature, developers still can have pride in what they have delivered. Even if no actual writing of code is involved, developers at Branch still complete work and demo the solution to business stakeholders. No one feels less because no "programming" was done to solve the problem.

At Insureco, executives are not expected to manage software vendor relationships (although they do manage other vendor relationships, such as with data vendors) because the technology organization likes to be in control of them. At Branch, the efficiency gains in having executives manage software vendor relationships (such as SaaS for the call center) means much tighter alignment, satisfaction, and accountability for those executives. It could be the case that many Insureco executives would refuse the responsibility to manage a software vendor because this would be beyond what should be expected of them, but that seems increasingly more untenable in the modern era. Just as an executive that "doesn't do email" probably isn't a great choice for a modern organization, so is an executive who is afraid of managing technology.

Summary: Achieving Better Business Outcomes

This chapter explains why Branch can achieve superior business outcomes to Insureco, leveraging the benefits of Serverless and other technical architectures in combination with a different organizational structure and business mentality.

Serverless enables Branch's technical employees to operate at a higher level than Insureco's because Branch employees are tackling problems that are more directly tied to business needs (such as helping to launch this state), compared to Insureco's technical employees, many of whom are working on infrastructure that is a requirement for but not directly needed by the business needs.

Branch's ability to operate at a higher level than Insureco, with less specialization, also makes it easier for Branch to have a different organizational structure and to align employees with business outcomes. Insureco's technical strategies rely primarily on particular technical architectures and tactics being implemented in isolation from the rest of the business.

Ultimately, Serverless is a critical component of an overall strategy that includes organizational and cultural elements, enabling Branch to deliver better business outcomes. Chapters 8 through 11 touch on how organizations can make all these changes in coordination.

References

[1] "Will big spending on computers guarantee profitability?" www.strassmann.com/pubs/datamation/datamation0297/index.html

[2] "Evolution begets Genesis begets Evolution." https://blog.gardeviance.org/2013/01/evolution-begets-genesis-begets.html

[3] Simon, Herbert. "The Architecture of Complexity." *Proceedings of the American Philosophical Society* 106, no. 6 (December 12, 1962: 467–482.http://links.jstor.org/sici?sici=0003-049X%2819621212%29106%3A6%3C467%3ATAOC%3E2.0.CO%3B2-1

[4] Alvarez, Cindy. *Lean Customer Development*. O'Reilly Media, 2017.

Chapter 8

Getting to Serverless

Up to this point, this book has focused on explaining what Serverless is and exploring its benefits. This chapter opens with a section on how organizations can adopt Serverless architectures to reap the benefits of this approach, even if their current state has no Serverless adoption at all. To start, the chapter explains how an organization needs to think and operate differently to make the change to Serverless.

Winning Hearts and Minds

The central challenge in making any significant organizational change is changing people's hearts and minds. People who have spent years taking pride in, being praised for, and earning bonuses based on how they do things are usually not able to turn on a dime and accept that doing things very differently would be better. This same kind of wariness has happened throughout time with technological advances such as electricity, the telephone, and cars. Even though new software development processes and tools emerge constantly, there is no continuing education in software development. Most software developers tend to use the processes and tools they learned early in their career instead of continually adopting new ones over time.

Nowhere is the maxim "Culture eats strategy for breakfast" more apparent than in rolling out large changes for software development practices. The strategy might be to make certain changes to improve speed, stability, and cost, but an organization's culture has been encoded into its existing systems. It's not just a matter of changing the hearts and minds of the developers; as odd as it sounds, it is also understanding how to change the culture of the code and systems themselves.

The first step in making any change is to define and get agreement on the primary optimization goal for software development teams. Once a clear and concise goal is established, metrics and compensation can be aligned with it. People can start executing on the tactics to achieve the goal. This section explains why the primary goal for optimization to achieve better software development outcomes is *maintainability* (that is, enabling high velocity of future changes) and delineating the key practices an organization needs to achieve that goal.

Optimizing for future change means that the systems that are set up are built in ways that make it easier for the developers who will be hired by the organization to run and modify those systems. This can mean choosing to buy services instead of building them. It can mean using common libraries and frameworks instead of writing them from scratch. It can mean organizing and documenting source code and configuration in ways that make it easy to teach how to modify and operate systems to people who are new to those systems.

Perhaps most important, it means assuming that the future developers of these systems will *not* be superstars or the same people who wrote it initially. Optimizing for maintainability includes an assumption that, in the future, the organization will require easy-to-understand, well-written, unburdened-by-massive-technical-debt source code and systems that can be maintained at a reasonable velocity.

Much has been written on how to write more maintainable source code. One excellent book on this topic is *Modern Software Engineering* by David Farley.[1] The author devotes an entire section to optimizing for managing complexity using *modularity*, *cohesion*, *separation of concerns*, and *abstraction*, and he addresses how to manage (and reduce) *coupling*. It is outside the scope of this book to discuss coding tactics in detail, but all these tactics (and more) are important tools in optimizing for maintainability.

Even if an organization is nearly perfect in how it writes code, it can severely suboptimize for maintainability by writing code if that code is undifferentiated for the organization and a licensable solution exists. Figure 8.1 provides a waterfall for implementing new functionality, in order of most maintainable to least, along with an explanation.

Don't Build

The most maintainable way to implement new functionality is to not implement the functionality at all. In the context of writing code, this is often called (feature) YAGNI (You Aren't Going to Need It).[2] This usually refers to part of a feature request that can be skipped for now because it's not immediately needed. However, the concept can be expanded more generally: As Steve Jobs once said, "I'm as proud

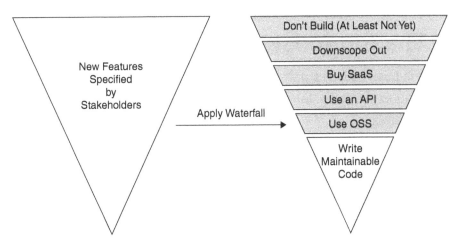

Figure 8.1 *How to Optimize for Future Change*

of many of the things we haven't done as the things we have done. Innovation is say-ing no to a thousand things."

Far too often, organizations build many things that are not needed or that were, in retrospect, a poor use of the time and effort it took to build them. Most organiza-tional leaders understand this and want to maximize the value of what the organiza-tion is paying to build. By having processes and a healthy level of skepticism about what the organization takes on to build, organizations will move faster on what is really needed and differentiated.

This is not to embrace the view that technology departments in organizations should be the departments of *no* (or arbitrary YAGNI). A more effective way to structure this healthy skepticism is for the organization to write down exactly what its differentiated values are and to require some structure and thought in requests to build, to make sure they're aligned with the goals the organization has as a whole. For example, at Branch, every request must go under one or more key objectives (which may or may not be formal objectives and key results [OKRs]) that are impor-tant for the company's future progress—perhaps "launch more insurance products," "improve conversion," or "improve operational efficiency." This provides an objec-tive context through which to examine and compare requests.

Building a culture of always asking, "What are we optimizing for?" is necessary to help ensure that what is being built makes sense for the organization. At Branch, the cultural "root" that explains this expectation is called the "top today" (see Figure 8.2).

The Top Today

- Hit Loss Ratio Target
- Launch Motorcycle
- Chatbot v2

Figure 8.2 *An Example of the Top Today*

The Top Today

We're all working together toward a common vision. So it's important that we're in sync, constantly communicating our top priorities.

It's critical that we constantly adjust our own priorities, according to what's at the top of the business's priority list. Once we've determined what is the top today, we need to proceed with a sense of urgency to ensure that it is accomplished.

Our clarity of priority enables us to capitalize on today's opportunities.

We give our full attention and energy to the top today and expect that, at the end of the day, there will be items of lesser urgency left for tomorrow.

We are honest with each other and ourselves about what we need to deliver on the top today, whether it be more help, time, or resources. Our commitment to communicate and collaborate enables us to build something special together.

It is important to not let a "top today" root justify never tackling systemic issues that cause slowness or pain in processes, such as technical debt, until they cause everything to come to a halt. Instead, the development team and other teams at Branch have specific strategies to "attach" systemic work, such as refactoring, to "top today" feature work. Branch resolves systemic problems when they exist within the systems or code that is being actively developed, as part of regular development work.

Downscope

The next most maintainable way to implement new functionality is to implement it in the simplest, least-effort (but sustainable) way necessary to move the ball forward. Sometimes this concept is confused with the minimum viable product (MVP) concept, but they are quite different. MVP is a model that seeks to build less functionality, but sometimes the simplest way to launch new functionality is to use something fully featured but requires some workarounds, such as a low-maintenance Rube Goldberg machine.

For example, when Branch was considering how to manage customer support and insurance underwriting review ticket management, one executive felt that custom software development was necessary because of some of the unique natures of the specific regulatory timeframes for certain work (and needing to make sure those timelines are always met). Instead of diving into the full specifications of what would have to be built, the stakeholders figured out how Zendesk could be configured to manage all the key requirements. The executive that pushed for the custom software development ultimately agreed that the ability to get up and running quickly with little execution risk was worth the pain of what they believed were peculiar workflows for insurance underwriters. Perhaps most tellingly, when it finally came time for Branch to leave Zendesk, it wasn't because of the workflows (which everyone had adapted to quite well), but rather because of something entirely different.

Downscoping effort does not always mean buying, though. It can often mean solving the problem through custom software development in a very different way. For example, someone might request the ability to fix a problem through an interface, but perhaps the problem can be automatically fixed as part of another process, which would eliminate the need for the interface at all. Every organization should have a relentless process for reducing implementation effort that uses all its available tools.

Building a culture of downscoping can be difficult in organizations where it has traditionally taken a significant time to build, including a long time to revise an initial build after launch. If software development teams can build downscoped requirements and release frequently, it becomes significantly easier to convince all stakeholders in an organization to accept a culture of downscoping. At Branch, the cultural root that explains to everyone how to think about downscoping is called "This is v1" (see Figure 8.3).

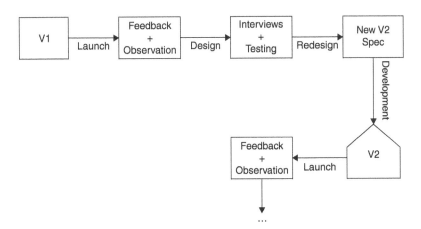

Figure 8.3 *"This Is v1" in Practice*

> ### This Is v1
>
> We live by the maxim that, when looking back, we should always be embarrassed by the v1 of what we've put into the world.
>
> Whenever we put something into the world, we give ourselves an opportunity to learn. That's how we improve and evolve. Don't let a fear of failure or imperfection stop you from trying.
>
> Look at each step as an opportunity. Don't let the smaller details stand in the way of getting to a powerful insight. Give it a shot—learn and iterate.
>
> These learnings become the stepping stones to the next play. Then we can look back at how far we've come and laugh.

Buy Off-the-Shelf SaaS

If it is necessary to implement a functionality, and the functionality has been downscoped and adjusted to decrease the effort it will take to get a v1 out the door, then the most maintainable choice is a service that the key business stakeholder can manage without day-to-day involvement from the technology department. Usually these are Software-as-a-Service (SaaS) subscriptions that many different organizations can use to solve similar problems to the one your organization is seeking to solve. SaaS subscriptions usually come with customer success teams, well-established onboarding and configuration support and documentation, and APIs that can be used to build integrations into other systems. If a SaaS option will manage a significant amount of the needed functionality, the best option is usually to identify whether the remaining functionality is necessary for v1, then design workarounds, and move forward with it.

It can be easy for organizations to assume that because they have a business-specific need and they build some custom software, every significant new functionality must be built as part of their custom software. However, when the scope of building the new functionality is 3 or more months (a general line at which development estimates tend be significant underestimates of actuals) and the functionality essentially exists with SaaS today, it is almost always a better choice to use the SaaS solution with light integration into the current custom software. *At the very least, this is the best approach to better learning customer needs.* Stakeholders are notoriously bad at knowing what they will want in a solution (which is one of the main reasons the Agile Manifesto[3] was created), so having something working as soon as possible and operating as a method for collecting better specification detail is a far better risk-adjusted option than spending enormous amounts of time in discovery, design, and development.

For small startups or extremely budget-constrained organizations, paying $10 to $150 per month per user (which is often how these solutions are priced) could be too expensive. However, in almost all cases, when the total costs of building and managing ongoing change are factored in, SaaS is cheaper by a significant margin.

Many organizations make it very hard to purchase SaaS, especially as a v1 experiment; paradoxically, they make it much easier to build or hire people to do inefficient manual tasks. This is usually less a cultural problem than a budgeting problem or a security or privacy problem.

The solution Branch has for the budgeting problem is a significant budget allocated to future SaaS/services that are to be evaluated in the coming year, without having to identify which services they are or determine those specific costs ahead of time. Executives at Branch strive to make it as easy as possible to evaluate new services so that employees feel pushed toward buying over asking for builds. (At the same time, Branch executives are maniacal about shutting off services if they're not used—one tactic here is to use virtual credit cards that end in 2 or 3 months to make sure recurring billing doesn't happen forever.)

The solution Branch has for security and privacy problems is a centralized information security office with a pragmatic third-party vendor evaluation process using Whistic.[4] Not every SaaS vendor will be an appropriate choice from a security perspective, but aligning the information security department with the organization's goals makes a significant difference. An information security office can drive extremely negative business results by making it much harder to use a SaaS solution, even if it is appropriate from a security standpoint, than to build internally. The cultural change discussed in this chapter needs to extend to the organization's approach to information security.

The worst-case scenario in having a "buy first" culture is that an organization can end up with many duplicate services that are managing similar work. This can involve overspending because of not making use of higher-usage discount tiers, and it can also mean that information is siloed in systems that not everyone has access to. This worst-case scenario is far better than building a bunch of different systems that need to be maintained. It can be managed through regular audits of SaaS in use and by working to move people from one system to another when it makes sense. In practice, though, having one team use LucidChart, another use Miro, and another use Visio for similar types of work has not presented significant problems at Branch.

Use a Managed-Service API

In some cases, buying SaaS cannot effectively solve the problem at hand, such as when having to make data easily searchable in an existing interface, build image thumbnails, or create invoice PDFs. Most developers search for sample code or libraries when confronted with requests for these types of integrated functionality, but in most cases, maintaining managed-service APIs is much easier than increasing the size and complexity of the organization-maintained codebase.

There is such an enormous discovery problem of "Is there an API to do that?" that the last section of this book (and the accompanying website) is a reference guide that lists a vast number of services that can be integrated into applications. Most developers and architects are not aware of many of these; if they knew the services existed, they likely would choose them more often.

The three previous examples are a great teaser for that section. Most organizations that have to build full text searching into their applications use Elasticsearch; even in semi-managed versions, this requires some amount of configuring systems, handling operational issues, needing to worry about patching and upgrading over time, and handling security, usually through a custom proxy. However, a fantastic full-text, fully managed service called Algolia[5] has at least 99% of Elasticsearch's functionality without any of its operational pains. It has a security model that allows for direct access from untrusted front ends that will work for the vast majority of use cases, allowing for sub-10 milliseconds searches, in most cases.

Most organizations that build image thumbnails these days have shifted to Serverless models, depositing image files into an object store such as Amazon S3 and then writing custom Serverless functions that run when new objects are saved and convert them using an open-source framework such as ImageMagick. A more maintainable option is to go with a service such as Cloudinary,[6] which can ingest images directly from untrusted clients and generates and caches all sorts of different transformations on images simply via URL parameters. Cloudinary also supports a robust set of security controls and integrates with human image filtering services. Thus, it is possible to completely outsource essentially everything that companies typically insource with respect to image processing: collection, human review for objectionable content, and watermarking/resizing of images.

Finally, and similarly to image processing, most organizations use an open-source library to generate PDFs based on some templating language, often HTML based. These solutions have the same operational challenges of handling image processing and running Elasticsearch: Organizations need operational teams to manage exceptions and failures; there are routinely pain points at scale, where having too many simultaneous requests causes problems; and bugs require painful manual operational partial "reruns." For PDF generation, DocRaptor[7] is a managed service that takes HTML with some custom CSS support specifically for print formatting, generates

PDFs, and even hosts them so that organizations don't have to worry about object storage and security around it. See Figure 8.4 for an example of how services like DocRaptor integrate with existing applications.

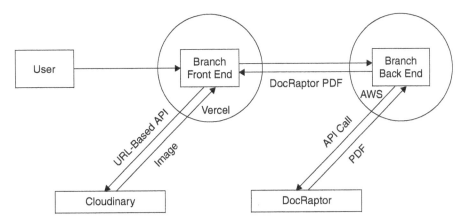

Figure 8.4 *An Example of How Branch Integrates DocRaptor and Cloudinary into Its Software*

Use Open-Source Libraries

When an organization needs to write custom code and no useful managed service can do the work, the next best option is to use open-source libraries instead of writing custom code. The most common open-source libraries that fit this model are frameworks such as React.js[8] and utility libraries such as Lodash[9].

In general, it is better to choose open-source libraries that are actively maintained (and you should support open-source maintainers!) and more popular than those that have not been updated in years and are not widely used. Writing custom code can sometimes make more sense than using an unmaintained, unpopular library.

Most software developers and architects do a great job of finding, choosing, and incorporating open-source libraries. The two biggest mistakes organizations make related to open-source libraries are not looking for managed-service APIs first, and then not looking long enough for an open-source library before writing custom code.

Write More Changeable Code

Finally, writing a significant amount of custom code is necessary for a particular solution, so the goal should be to make the code more maintainable. This tactic is often summarized as "write less code," which can be useful but is overly reductive.

Many developers immediately chafe at a "write less code" directive, pointing out that some of the worst code can be found when developers minimize lines of code (as with the obfuscated Perl contest[10] run from 1996 to 2000). David Farley's *Modern Software Engineering* is a great resource that walks through the tactics of writing more maintainable code, which does not necessarily involve writing fewer lines of code. He gives great examples of how slightly more lines of code can be more maintainable because they reduce coupling; he also points out when Don't Repeat Yourself (DRY) is best used to reduce lines of code and when it shouldn't be used (thus yielding more lines of code).

At a macro level, organizations should acknowledge that orders of magnitude more code is harder to maintain than orders of magnitude less code. Organizations should seek to reduce the orders of magnitude of code they are generating. The previously mentioned tactics (not writing code at all, using managed-service APIs, and using open-source libraries) reduce the amount of code written by orders of magnitude. When code actually needs to be written, optimizing for maintainability means focusing on what an average developer will be able to understand and designing for different developers to be able to simultaneously work on different parts of the codebase.

The Metrics That Matter

Even if an organization has adopted a Serverless-friendly culture and mindset, focusing on maintainability and relentlessly building only what needs to be built, a focus on the wrong metrics can sabotage effective software development. In contrast, a focus on the right metrics can help position an organization so that transitions from traditional architectures to Serverless architectures are much easier to do and easier to celebrate.

Dr. Nicole Forsgren, Gene Kim, and Jez Humble have written the definitive book on software development metrics: *Accelerate: The Science of Lean Software and DevOps: Building and Scaling High Performing Technology Organizations*.[11] The authors lay out the four metrics that top-performing development organizations use, delineate what values are sufficient to be successful, and explain why the metrics are the correct ones. Figure 8.5 is a recap of the metrics they outline in *Accelerate* and how they enable organizations to more effectively move to Serverless.

Change Lead Time (Cycle Time)

Change Lead Time (more commonly called Cycle Time) is defined in *Accelerate* as the time between code being committed and running in production. Since the introduction of this metric, a fair amount of discussion has arisen over how best to think about when code counts as being "committed," as well as whether it is better to break this metric into submetrics.

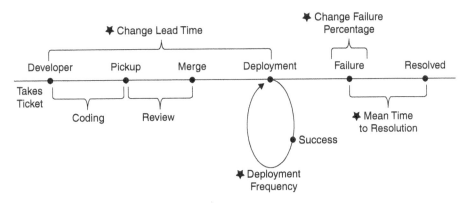

Figure 8.5 *An Illustration of the Metrics That Matter, on a Timeline*

LinearB[12], a SaaS product that automatically calculates development metrics from data in source codes repositories, breaks Cycle Time into Coding (first commit on a branch to pull request opened), Pickup (time it takes for someone to do a first code review), Review (time from first code review to merge), and Deploy (time it takes from merge to being live in production). LinearB also publishes its guidelines for the best values for each of these: To be Elite, Coding should take less than 24 hours, Pickup less than 12 hours, Review less than 4 hours, and Deploy less than 6 hours.

It is important to note that doing work in very small pieces is critical to successfully hitting these targets. If most pull requests in an organization are hundreds of lines of code, they are not likely to hit these targets. On the other hand, if organizations are using feature flags and breaking work into very small pieces, it is much easier to hit them.

Regardless of whether an organization qualifies as Elite on these metrics, simply focusing on getting code into production quickly once completed is a far better focus for an organization than counting story points (or, even worse, lines of code) or looking at burn up/burn down charts. Having alignment in moving things into production regularly and without unnecessary delay enables an organization to accept the downscoping of specifications, because updates can come quickly.

Deployment Frequency

Along the same lines, and with the same motivations as decreasing cycle time is deployment frequency. Top-performing software development organizations focus on deploying at least once (but ideally, many times) per week. Note that this is an explicit rejection of how many enterprises approach agile software development, running 2-week sprints with a release at the end of each sprint. *Accelerate* does a great job of explaining why releasing every 2 weeks is the hallmark of a suboptimal development process and why an organization should definitely focus on this metric.

It is important to note that automated testing and code review are both critical to organizations being able to release multiple times per week. It is not possible to run effective, modern software development without automated testing. Many services and tools make automated testing easier to implement than ever, and this is no longer an optional practice. More debate centers on how important mandatory, universal code review is for organizations today than on automated testing, but in this author's experience, code review keeps every developer honest and improves the quality of all software development.

Change Fail Percentage

When an organization pushes multiple production releases per week, even with highly effective automated testing, some of the releases will contain bugs that need to be fixed immediately. Some bugs can be found only in production environments because perfect simulations of production are impossible. A certain amount of the time, then, there will be a need to make a change in response to a production deploy. In *Accelerate*, the authors explain that top-performing organizations have a change fail percentage of less than 50%.

For most engineering managers, that is a shocking statement because 50% seems so high. Many organizations build brutal roadblocks that slow down development and release to production over any kind of significant bug going into the production environment. However, the benefit of a development organization that can release to production quickly is that problems can be resolved quickly (see the next metric). Allowing for errors is therefore a key aspect of effective software development.

At Branch, deployments never completely take down entire systems; automated tests ensure that the vast majority of functionality is working correctly before production deploys. But bugs occasionally are released into production, usually affecting a small subset of users, and need to be fixed quickly. One surprising point, though, is that most of these bugs are not found immediately after release; most are found after a subsequent release. Frequent releases and automated testing reduces the scope impact of bugs, requiring a change in how bugs are treated and handled—usually not by rolling back but rather by rolling forward.

Mean Time to Recovery

Finally, if organizations are to have bugs that need quick resolution, it is important to measure how quickly those fixes are deployed to production. This is the *mean time to recovery (MTTR)*. Ideally, an organization should have an MTTR of less than 5 hours.

With Serverless infrastructures, it is important to think about MTTR in the context of managed service downtime. When an application is down because it relies upon a managed service to be up (whether this is cloud infrastructure or a high-level critical service, such as payments), it is still down. Organizations should be sure they are making good vendor choices for critical services by reviewing historic uptime statistics and understanding escalation paths when services are not performing appropriately.

Ready to Begin

Once an organization has the right philosophy and metrics and has worked to adjust its cultural norms to align with the values described in this chapter, it is ready to begin moving to Serverless. The next two chapters address the key tactics to use to start moving code and architecture to Serverless, as well as to start moving the people who have been building and maintaining the "serverful" architectures.

Summary: Organizational Steps to Serverless

This book has discussed the concept of Serverless and its benefits. This current chapter focuses on how organizations can adopt Serverless architectures, even if they have no previous Serverless adoption. The chapter explains that organizations need to change their thinking and operating methods to make such a transition.

The first change that an organization needs to make is to align every stakeholder in the organization on the business benefits the organization expects to achieve by changing its technical architecture. The organization also needs to have conversations with stakeholders to answer their questions. Once the organization has an initial understanding of *why*, it can start applying the framework toward software development that was laid out in this chapter: don't build, downscope, buy off-the-shelf SaaS, use a managed-service API, use open-source libraries, and write changeable code. When writing software, organizations should focus on the metrics that matter: change lead time, deployment frequency, change fail percentage, and mean time to recovery.

Organizations that adopt these practices can begin to tackle their existing codebases and transition them to be more easily and efficiently changed.

References

[1] Farley, David. *Modern Software Engineering: Doing What Works to Build Better Software Faster.* Addison-Wesley Professional, 2021.

[2] "Yagni." https://martinfowler.com/bliki/Yagni.html

[3] www.agilemanifesto.org/

[4] www.whistic.com/

[5] www.algolia.com/

[6] www.cloudinary.com/

[7] www.docraptor.com/

[8] www.reactjs.org/

[9] www.lodash.com/

[10] "Obfuscated Perl Contest." https://en.wikipedia.org/wiki/Obfuscated_Perl_Contest

[11] Forsgren, Nicole, et al. *Accelerate: The Science Behind DevOps: Building and Scaling High Performing Technology Organizations.* IT Revolution Press, 2018.

[12] https://linearb.io/

Chapter 9

Iterative Replacement

Once an organization has decided that it wants to build software Serverlessly and has enlisted a cultural commitment to making that change, it can move forward. However, if an organization chooses the wrong tactics to implement Serverless architectures, it will be doomed to fail. The information in this chapter comes from experts who have seen many failed and successful rewrites of software. This chapter explains how the traditional knife-edge cutover rewrite is almost never successful, describes an iterative replacement strategy, and discusses why organizations should follow that alternative strategy to maximize their chance of success. The references at the end of this chapter provide further key reading for anyone embarking on even a partial rewrite.

The Knife-Edge Cutover Doesn't Work

When facing a decision to rebuild software, most organizations default to a knife-edge cutover strategy, in which the replacement software is developed separately from the current software and then, at a date in the future, the replacement is turned on and hopefully magically replaces the older software.

The knife-edge cutover is an extremely high-risk strategy that rarely works for any non-trivially sized piece of software. The general idea is to build a complete replacement for the existing software, migrate all the data, and then, in one day, switch all the users from the older software to the newer software. The usual plan is to freeze all new development on the existing software while building its replacement, to maximize the number of developers working on the rewrite.

However, the knife-edge cutover does not work, for many reasons. The least obvious reason is that the existing codebase has significant business logic that is impossible to understand properly by rewriting specifications from scratch and reading existing code. Instead, organizations that rewrite find themselves repeatedly relearning and reimplementing complex business logic. This is unavoidable and makes sense—complex business logic implemented in code is exceedingly difficult to get right on the first try, and it wasn't implemented correctly the first time in the existing code, either. The magnitude of the number of business logic errors that will happen if an organization tries all at once to put into production a large codebase that has not been run is such that famous software developer Joel Spolsky wrote a broadly popular piece in which he argued that no organization should ever rewrite any software.[1]

Beyond the painful process of rediscovering encoded business logic during the rewrite process, feature and specification changes will continue to happen, regardless of how badly the organization wants to freeze features. Users of any important software have expectations today that bugs will be fixed and software will be improved, and organizations that serve those users cannot afford to irritate users with prolonged periods of time without new releases. Achieving a feature freeze is no more likely to succeed than suggesting to someone who owes a lot of money to simply stop spending money on anything (including rent and food) until the debt is repaid. Instead, the rewrite will have to constantly chase a changing specification.

Yet another reason the knife-edge cutover does not work is that it will take much longer than anyone expects; the likelihood that the executives running the project will still be working for the organization when it actually completes thus approaches zero. Software estimation is notoriously difficult, and as the scope of a project increases, the specification becomes less specific ("copy existing functionality of this application" is not specific!). As the specification changes over time, the accuracy of estimates decreases precipitously. The author of this book has witnessed dozens of attempted software rewrites, none of which were completed even a year beyond the amount of time initially estimated.

Despite the nearly unanimous opposition to full rewrites with knife-edge cutovers among experienced software development leaders, many organizations continue to pursue them as a primary strategy. This is because, for many other projects that require architecture and construction, it is not possible to iteratively change them into something else. If someone desires a long one-story ranch home, transforming a narrow three-story walk-up over time is not a preferred strategy. Yet software is conducive to iterative changes, and in software, making smaller changes rapidly is preferable. The next sections explain that strategy, show why it is better than the knife-edge cutover, and detail how it applies in moving to Serverless architectures.

What Is Iterative Replacement?

In a 2004 blog post, Martin Fowler outlined the now-canonical strategy of how to rewrite software systems, using the analogy of how strangler fig plants take over trees, stealing all their nutrients and sometimes eventually causing the tree to die.[2] Birds often drop strangler fig seeds onto trees. The seeds land in nooks and slowly grow downward and upward, taking nutrients from the tree to fuel the growth. Eventually, the exterior of the tree is covered by the strangler fig. This is a much better way to think about building a new software system to replace an old one: Start small, make it self-sustaining from the beginning, and grow on top of the existing structure.

For a variety of reasons, the term *iterative replacement* is more accurate and illustrative of this practice (not to mention less violent!), so that is the term this book uses. Iterative replacement involves several key practices: establishing an event interception (Fowler's term) to iteratively build in small pieces, providing backward compatibility by reverse-migrating state, building all new features in only a single place, and accepting that the replacement could take a very long time.

Event Interception (Reverse Proxy)[3]

The first step in any iterative replacement project is to intercept all traffic to the system being replaced. Usually this is done with a reverse proxy or something similar— for example, in replacing a back-end API, sending all traffic to another system that will route some traffic to the original API and route other traffic to the newly written system(s) (see Figure 9.1). For this chapter, the term *reverse proxy* is used to refer to the system put in front of the existing system, intercepting all events that go to the existing system.

The reverse proxy is critical to a successful iterative replacement, for many reasons. First, it is usually not an enormous project to stand up the reverse proxy. The most significant impact on the existing systems will be seen and felt immediately through the additional latency that the reverse proxy adds. In most cases, it should

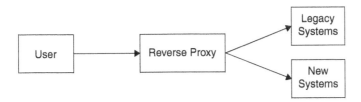

Figure 9.1 *A Simple Reverse Proxy*

be possible to keep that additional latency to less than 50ms, especially if using an edge-based solution to run it (such as Cloudflare CDN[4] or AWS CloudFront with Lambda@Edge[5]). Getting the reverse proxy up in a few weeks and letting everyone know that this is the biggest impact they are going to see for the whole project is a huge win for everyone; it's much less risky than keeping developers hiding in a closet for 18 months or more, hoping that what they deliver will magically work to replace everything.

Second, the reverse proxy enables smaller chunks of code to be rewritten than without it. This is because developers and architects working with an existing system have to work within the constraints of the existing system. The lens and capability of a reverse proxy enables them to see how the code can be broken up much more easily.

For example, if Insureco has one million lines of code that calculate rates for its home and auto insurance products, with significant technical debt and poor separation of concerns, developers at Insureco are going to have a tough time thinking about how to break that up into pieces. However, with a reverse proxy, it is much simpler to identify just one case for rating—for example, only one driver and one car needing an insurance price in Wyoming. The reverse proxy can send requests for one driver and one car in Wyoming to new code and then send all other requests to the old code. This can then repeat forever, ensuring that the team is making frequent small deployments so that every week more use cases are running on the new code.

Third, the reverse proxy enables running canaries and rolling back easily. The concept of a canary in software development involves identifying whether new code might be bad quickly even though it has been run only a small number of times in production. A reverse proxy can easily implement sending a small portion of traffic to new code (as in the previous case, sending only 1% of all one driver, one car, Wyoming auto rate calls to the new code, to start).

The reverse proxy makes iterative replacements possible, allows them to be scoped into small chunks, and takes an enormous amount of risk out of any replacement project.

State-Harmonizing Synchronization (Asset Capture)[6]

When making small, iterative replacements, it is usually necessary to have some synchronization of state between two separate systems that store state. In the previous example of splitting up insurance rating code, the existing rating system can store calculation results in a database that has been labeled "legacy" and needs to be replaced as part of the larger project (for example, moving from a relational database in a data center to a Serverless cloud database such as AWS DynamoDB). However, it might not be possible to store some of the results in the new database and others in the old database because enough other code assumes that all results are still either in the old database or in the new database. In these situations, it is necessary to be able to migrate data from the old to the new and also reverse migrate it from the new to the old.

Fowler calls this concept asset capture, to invoke a mental model of the data being modified as a distinct asset that must exist cohesively wherever it needs to be. Doing this efficiently requires significant planning and understanding of the existing systems (although no more than is required to know how to rewrite all the functionality). One effective strategy here is to apply the reverse proxy concept to code that accesses both old and new data and then either modify it, ideally centralized and reused so that it knows where to look for particular records, or just have it search both and combine results.

Build New Once

A significant benefit to the iterative replacement strategy is that new features do not need to be built twice. While doing iterative replacement, new features can be built either as entirely new code using new systems or as part of refactoring older code. This takes away two huge pain points of knife-edge cutovers: the initial decision to not build any new features, and then the requirements that come anyway to build new features because the rewrite is taking longer than expected or the new features are too important.

The easiest way to build new features is to build them in compliance with the new way that they should be done and to use the reverse proxy to direct traffic to them. However, sometimes the new feature needs to be deeply integrated with existing code, and that existing code might also be tightly bound to an existing database or datastore. In these cases, it is worth treating the new feature as a new feature plus a refactor and allocating additional development time to do the work.

A Very Long Time

One of the biggest mistakes that organizations make in planning to replace an existing system is the assumption that they will shut down the existing system in relatively short order. A companion mistake that often comes along with this assumption is also assigning significant cost benefits or velocity benefits to the shutdown event. Both tend to prioritize work at the very end of the replacement process that has an extremely poor return on investment to the organization, but the organization tends to force through that work anyhow because of accounting rules or employee bonuses.

In other words, organizations often take a mental shortcut and assume that the most significant benefits of moving from an old system to a new system happen *after everything is completely shut off in the old system.* Usually, however, once most functionality is running in the new system, the organization has captured most of the benefits. The 80/20 rule applies just as well here as it does in most places: Often 80% of the benefit is achieved in the first 20% of the work, and the remaining 20% of the benefit takes 80% of the remaining time. Nothing is wrong with leaving a small amount of infrequently used, low-value cases in the old system for an extended period of time in order to focus on adding new features and immediately taking advantage of the new velocity benefits.

The best consideration is this: Assume that most of existing systems have been replaced, most of the benefits (faster development velocity, lower cost of mainte-nance, and happier people) have been achieved, and that some lesser-used function-ality in the old code remains, with lower availability and uptime requirements on the existing system. Because of the lower requirements, running the existing system has become a lot cheaper and easier. At this point in time, is it necessary to completely shut down and remove the old system, or might it be better to let it keep running and direct efforts toward building new functionality?

The much better risk mitigation strategy in replacement plans is to assume that the old systems will be downsized and significantly reduced in importance but that they might not go away—ever. The metrics to celebrate should be the ones driving the reasons for the replacement project, such as shorter cycle time or more releases per week.

Iterative Replacement to Serverless Architectures

A migration to a Serverless architecture works very well both as the core driver and as a part of a systems replacement project. Several key differences exist between iter-ative replacement projects with and without a Serverless mindset: up-front research on managed services, databases and datastores, and Serverless used as the infrastruc-ture for scaffolding the rewrite.

Up-Front Research

The first task any team contemplating a rewrite with a Serverless mindset should do is to identify the managed services that will be used in the new application architec-ture. (Note that the appendix is an excellent resource for identifying useful services.) If teams understand at the beginning which services can be used, the rewrite will be far more efficient; otherwise, a lot of time likely will be wasted developing code that need not be written. Additionally, it will be harder to throw away that code later, even though it is a sunk cost.

Note that this kind of up-front research is often disregarded as not being sufficiently agile and sometimes seen in violation of the You Aren't Going to Need It (YAGNI) principle discussed in Chapter 8, "Getting to Serverless." However, because so little code is used when leveraging managed services, the things that you aren't going to need do not carry with them the liability of having been built in custom code that must be maintained. Thus, there is immense value in identifying services that can be used, validating how they can work together, and ensuring that they meet necessary requirements before beginning any replacement project. If they happen to come with additional features that do not seem like they will be used initially, that is usually a benefit instead of a downside; there is a chance that they will be needed down the road because other customers who needed the same core features wanted them as well.

One effective strategy for identifying what managed services should be considered is to imagine rearchitecting the entire application or system as if it were to be built greenfield, with no constraints. This strategy is often a poor choice when iteratively replacing an existing system with custom code because it is too much of a fantasy: The existing stack and code organization will have a significant impact on how it can be replaced. With a Serverless approach, it is often possible to identify a managed service that can handle complete functionality (for example, using Algolia for search) for 70 to 80% of the user stories necessary for current and near-future organizational needs. This can then trigger a short amount of development work with the reverse proxy so that 70 to 80% is pulled out of incoming requests and redirected to the managed service, usually with a little glue code.

The overall impact of identifying managed services that can be adopted as part of a larger code modernization project accelerates the rate at which code can be retired, increases overall operational availability, and decreases the amount of code that needs to be maintained. In other words, bringing a transition to Serverless into a larger rewrite project usually means that the project completes cheaper, faster, and better.

Databases and Datastores

Traditional systems often have one large central database. Serverless architectures often use multiple databases and datastores for different use cases and because different managed services are used. For example, Branch uses DynamoDB as a key-value store for insurance transactions, PostgreSQL as a structured database for certain lookup tables, Amazon S3 for storing insurance documents, Redis as a cache, and Algolia for searching.

If the planning for a rewrite identifies opportunities to use multiple services that will store data, it can make the rewrite easier to adopt each one in a separate phase and to migrate the canonical datastore for writes last. For example, imagine that an organization has SQL Server databases that it uses for blob (file) storage and all transactional queries, and is planning to move to Azure Storage, CosmosDB, and Algolia. In this case, the move to CosmosDB should be done last. Algolia can be set up to index against SQL Server, and then front-end application logic can be changed to query Algolia. Azure Storage can be set up to store new files, application logic can look in both SQL Server blob tables and Azure Storage for files, and then the files can be migrated over gradually, if desired. Finally, when it is time to move tabular data to CosmosDB, it is straightforward to have Algolia index from Cosmos instead of SQL Server.

Good opportunities also might arise to use managed services as proxies for data. In the previous example, Algolia is essentially used as a read proxy for information in the database. Moving as many queries as possible to Algolia instead of directly to SQL Server makes the transition from SQL Server to CosmosDB less risky because there are fewer ways SQL Server is being used directly.

However, beware of a common desire to build custom-code database proxy services. These were popular ideas when organizations started building microservices: Instead of accessing a database's API directly, applications would interact with a custom-built intermediary service that would have business-specific logic. The challenge with these services is that they often end up being significant bottlenecks to software development velocity because every way that anyone wants to access any datastore must modify the intermediary service. This high amount of traffic on the intermediary service leads to bugs and incidents, which lead to stricter controls on modifying the service, which slows down all development.

The preferred approach is to have applications interact directly with datastore APIs instead of building an intermediate, bespoke data interaction API. Use the selection of datastores, as well as the configuration options within the datastores, to enforce necessary business rules. Additionally, if common functions are executed against the datastores (for example, Branch has a function to determine the current installment payment plan for a given policy), they should live in common libraries or be their own service. However, they should not be part of a strategy that forbids direct datastore access for other queries.

Scaffolding

Finally, a move to a Serverless architecture presents an opportunity to use Serverless architectures within the scaffolding that is used to reverse-proxy traffic to new and old code. An organization might choose to use AWS API Gateway as a reverse proxy, which would give the organization a good understanding of how API Gateway works from the very beginning of the project. On the other hand, an organization might choose to use a service such as Cloudflare, which manages connectivity from DNS on down to custom code execution at the edge, as its reverse proxy and a way to route traffic for the foreseeable future.

An organization might also choose to use managed services not just for the source of primary web traffic, but also as a replacement for specific significant bespoke systems that can now move. For example, an organization might decide to retire its identity and access management code in favor of a service such as Auth0. If that is a major part of the rewrite, it would likely make sense to do that migration first and do the integration work in the legacy code; this would enable the new code to also use Auth0 (instead of the legacy authentication code) and leverage authenticated access more quickly.

Ultimately, a significant amount of planning and understanding which managed services an organization is going to use provides opportunities for rewrites to go more quickly and with less risk than they would otherwise.

Summary: Iterative Replacement

An organization that has decided to build software Serverlessly must choose the right tactics to implement it successfully. A knife-edge cutover rewrite, which is a traditional approach, is almost never successful. An iterative replacement strategy is recommended instead, in which the new Serverless architecture is gradually introduced while the old one is phased out. This approach maximizes the chance of success.

Iterative replacement is a well-documented and well-understood process. Moving to a Serverless architecture can be fairly straightforward because of the variety of managed services, such as API gateways and database migration services, that fill key needs of an iterative replacement strategy.

References

[1] "Things You Should Never Do, Part I." www.joelonsoftware.com/2000/04/06/things-you-should-never-do-part-i/

[2] "StranglerFigApplication." https://martinfowler.com/bliki/StranglerFigApplication.html

[3] "EventInterception." https://martinfowler.com/bliki/EventInterception.html

[4] https://workers.cloudflare.com/

[5] https://aws.amazon.com/lambda/edge/

[6] "AssetCapture." https://martinfowler.com/bliki/AssetCapture.html

Chapter 10

Training and Continuing Education

An organization that is culturally ready and has a viable plan to adopt Serverless still needs to produce a plan for training, hiring, and continuing education for all its technical (and some nontechnical) employees. This chapter walks through the key personnel needs that will change, along with effective strategies to improve current employee effectiveness and hire new talent more easily.

Jobs and People Will Change

When moving to Serverless, a number of jobs that have been critical to have in-house become increasingly lighter in terms of workload. The types of jobs in this category include building and maintaining physical servers, virtual servers, and containers (servers); creating and applying configuration to servers; selecting and installing software on servers; patching operating systems and server software; optimizing and scaling servers; monitoring and responding to issues identified in monitoring; and training and assisting other teams in preparing software to be deployed and updated on servers.

However, Charity Majors, a longtime leader and expert in operations and the founder of Honeycomb, explains that the central movement of these jobs under Serverless is not that they disappear, but that they move to more automated and strategic roles. Much like virtualization significantly increased the number of servers that any individual systems administrator could oversee, Serverless dramatically increases how much of the organization an individual operations employee can influence. Serverless allows operations staff to be more strategic and all encompassing, through a much simpler collection of rules than those necessary when server, container, and software management is required. Under Serverless, operations staff can focus on access rules that custom code has with other custom code and managed services instead of worrying about many exploits through operating systems and web server daemons.

The New Ops Jobs[1] (Excerpt)

By Charity Majors

Infrastructure, ops, devops, systems engineering, sysadmin, infraops, SRE, platform engineering. As long as I've been doing computers, these terms have been effectively synonymous. If I wanted to tell someone what my job was, I could throw out any one of them and expect to be understood.

Every tech company had a software engineering team that built software and an operations team that built infrastructure for running that software. At some point in the past decade, they would have renamed this operations team to devops or SRE, but whatever the name, that was my team and those were my people.

But unless you're an infrastructure company, infrastructure is not your mission. Which means that every second you devote to infrastructure work—and every engineer you devote to infrastructure problems—is a distraction from your core goals.

These days, you increasingly have a choice. Sure, you can build all that internal expertise, but every day more of it is being served up via API on a silver platter.

Does this mean that operations is no longer important, no longer necessary? Far from it. Operability, resiliency, and reliability have never been more important. The role of operations engineers is changing fast, and the role is bifurcating along the question of infrastructure. In the future, people who would formerly have called themselves operations engineers (or devops engineers) will get to choose between a role that emphasizes building infrastructure software as a service and a role that uses their infrastructure expertise to help teams of engineers ship software more effectively and efficiently...generally, by building as little infrastructure as possible.

If your heart truly beats for working on infrastructure problems, you're in luck! There are more of those than ever. Go join an infrastructure company. Try one of the many companies—AWS, Azure, all the many developer tooling companies—whose mission consists of building infrastructure software, being the best in the world at infrastructure, and selling that expertise to other companies. There are roles for software engineers who enjoy building infrastructure solutions as a service, and there are even specialist ops roles for running and operating that infrastructure at scale or for administering those data services at scale. Whether you are a developer or not, working alone or in a team, Azure DevOps training can help you organize the way you plan, create, and deliver software.

Otherwise, embrace the fact that your job consists of building systems to enable teams of engineers to ship software that creates core business value, which means home brewing as little infrastructure as possible. And what's left?

Vendor Engineering

Effectively outsourcing components of your infrastructure and weaving them together into a seamless whole involves a great deal of architectural skill and domain expertise. This skill set is both rare and incredibly undervalued, especially considering how pervasive the need for it is. Think about it. If you work at a large company, dealing with other internal teams should feel like dealing with vendors. And if you work at a small company, dealing with other vendors should feel like dealing with other teams.

Anyone who wants a long and vibrant career in SRE leadership would do well to invest some energy into areas like these:

Learn to evaluate vendors and their products effectively. Ask piercing, probing questions to gauge compatibility and fit. Determine which areas of friction you can live with and which are dealbreakers.

Learn to calculate and quantify the cost of your time and labor, as well as your team's. Be ruthless about shedding as much labor as possible in order to focus on your core business.

Learn to manage the true cost of ownership and to advocate and educate internally for the right solution, particularly by managing up to execs and finance folks.

Product Engineering

One of the great tragedies of infrastructure is how thoroughly most of us managed to evade the past 20+ years of lessons in managing products and learning how to work with designers. It's no wonder most infrastructure tools require endless laborious trainings and certifications. They simply weren't built like modern products for humans.

I recommend a crash course. Embed yourself within a B2B or B2C feature delivery team for a bit. Learn their rhythms, learn their language, soak up some of their instincts. You'll need them to balance and blend your instincts for architectural correctness, scaling patterns, and firefighting.

You don't have to become an expert in shipping features. But you should learn the elements of relationship building the way a good product manager does. And you must learn enough about the product lifecycle that you can help debug and divert teams whose roadmaps are hopelessly intertwined and whose roadmaps are grinding to a halt.

Sociotechnical Systems Engineering

The irreducible core of the SRE/devops skill set increasingly revolves around crafting and curating efficient, effective sociotechnical feedback loops that enable and empower engineers to ship code—to move swiftly, with confidence. Your job is not to say no or throw up roadblocks; it's to figure out how to help them get to yes.

Start with embracing releases. Lean hard into the deploy pipeline. The safest diff is the smallest diff, and you should ship automatically and compulsively. Optimize tests and CI/CD so that deploys happen automatically upon merge to main, so that a single merge set gets deployed at a time, there are no human gates, and everything goes live automatically within a few minutes of a developer committing code. This is your holy grail, and most teams are nowhere near there.

Design and optimize on-call rotations that load-balance the effort fairly and sustainably and won't burn people out. Apply the appropriate amount of pressure on management to devote enough time to reliability and fixing things instead of just shipping new features. Hook up the feedback loops so that the people who are getting alerted are the ones empowered and motivated to fix the problems that are paging them. Ideally, you should page the person who made the change, every time.

Foster a culture of ownership and accountability while promulgating blamelessness throughout the org. Welcome engineers into production, and help them navigate production waters happily and successfully.

Managing the Portfolio of Technical Investments

Operability is the longest-term investment and primary source of technical debt, so no one is better positioned to help evaluate and amortize those risks than ops engineers. Writing code is effectively free, compared to the gargantuan resources it takes to run that code and tend to it over the years.

Get excellent at migrations. Leave no trailing, stale remnants of systems behind to support—those are a terrible drain on the team. Surface this energy drain to decision makers instead of letting it silently fester.

Hold the line against writing any more code than is absolutely necessary or adding any more tools than are necessary. Your line is, "What is the maintenance plan for this tool?"

Educate and influence. Lobby for the primacy of operability. Take an interest in job ladders and leveling documents. No one should be promoted to senior engineering levels unless they write and support operable services.

This world is changing fast, and these changes are accelerating. Ops is everybody's job now. Many engineers have no idea what this means and have absorbed the lingering cultural artifacts of terror. It's our job to fix the terror we ops folks instilled. We must find ways to reward curiosity, not punish it.

Near-Term Job Changes

Although organizations are in the process of iteratively replacing legacy systems with Serverless ones, there are also iterative moves that people in specific roles can take to learn new skills that have greater strategic impact. This section outlines a few natural opportunities to make these transitions.

Systems Administrator to Application Operations

Over the past decade, systems administrators have increasingly learned how to use configuration files (such as Terraform and Helm) to define and deploy infrastructure instead of manually deploying everything. As an organization increasingly shifts to Serverless architectures, the tasks of defining the "infrastructure" as code become much simpler and can often be done by software developers because of their simplicity (for example, YAML files for the Serverless Application Model [SAM]).

This shift in organizational need opens the ability for systems administrators to focus on Serverless application operations: organization-specific monitoring, incident detection, and remediation. In Serverless architectures, it is rarely necessary to worry about any hardware or scaling issues, but there are always issues that are specific to certain use cases (often edge cases). Setting up structured logging in applications, especially in a high-cardinality observability service such as Honeycomb,[2] enables issues to be identified that no one had any time or capacity to find and resolve before.

Database Administrator to Database Designer and Catalog Manager

Database administrators have focused on database design and optimization for decades. The design skills are still extremely useful (but usually different) in Serverless architectures, with the increasing adoption of NoSQL databases such as DynamoDB that have vastly different design and management patterns. (Alex Debrie's *The DynamoDB Book*[3] is a must-read for details on how best to build on DynamoDB).

But even with new design requirements, Serverless databases need extraordinarily little optimization or maintenance after initial setup, beyond designing for new features or access patterns, or the occasional restore. This frees up database administrators to focus on adding value to the organization by helping drive the data into a data lake and building effective data catalogs for analysts to consume the data through a reporting system.

Transitioning Titles

Organizations that have roles that are tied to a specific technology that is on its way to being sunset, such as Oracle Database Administrator or Kubernetes Administrator, need to think through how to transition the role title and redefine the core responsibilities so that they do not lose valuable employees necessary to maintain existing systems through the period of iterative replacement. It is sometimes difficult for people to want to give up a primary responsibility doing something different from how they have identified their value (as with someone who knows a specific technology). It may be easier to both (a) create the new role that encompasses the existing responsibilities and (b) find someone new to set up for success in that role instead of helping an existing employee find a new work identity.

The next sections discuss how organizations can help employees find new work identities, even for those who do not particularly welcome change. Even though a big shift in technical architecture might take their breath away, they have significant understanding of the organization and deserve the opportunity to come along.

How to (Re)train Your Workforce

Training is conceptually simple: Identify valuable resources that will explain how to do the specific job, and send employees through them: books, online courses, in-person workshops, and/or conferences. However, as with organizational change, the difficult part involves culture and identity. People who see their value as a more general contribution to the overall organization and who believe they should be continually learning new things will have a much easier time with a move to Serverless than people who see their value tied to the tactics they do today.

The best way, then, to introduce changes in titles and responsibilities is to first have an employee base that wants to change in alignment with what will work best for the organization. An African proverb says, "If you want to go fast, go alone. If you want to go far, go together." Moving an organization along a trajectory of meaningful change requires everyone going together, often needing to realize each of the cognitive steps along the way to get to the end outcome.

Retraining around Serverless often focuses only on operations jobs. However, software developers also need to understand that Serverless requires different practices than traditional architectures, even if the programming language is the same. To be an effective developer of Serverless applications, developers should take the time to learn how their code is built and run on whichever cloud platform or managed service is handling its operations. Many developers that are accustomed to running and debugging code locally try to force that practice with Serverless development, when it could be much more effective to debug remotely against a deployed version of the application.

If an organization is moving from physical servers in a data center to a completely Serverless architecture, it could be necessary to take a significant amount of time with all the key administrators, developers, and architects to build example infrastructures in all the different major ways that have been used over the past decades: Build an application on a managed hosting provider, see how that infrastructure is difficult to manage, replicate the operating system and application configurations, and scale. Build via the console on a cloud provider, and investigate the complexity; see how doing something like running out of space on the database server causes everything to crash and then requires a painful recovery process. Build out a Kubernetes cluster and understand its massive complexity. People who have hands-on experience with each of these and their pain points will be able to more effectively build out modern architectures and will be more appreciative of their benefits.

A New Hiring Advantage

When an organization is running Serverless applications, it increasingly has a hiring advantage over competitors: It can more easily hire junior developers and also turn front-end developers into full-stack developers. Branch mainly hires junior developers, and most developers at Branch started their software development careers at Branch. Junior developers also have a significant advantage when building Serverless applications: They don't have to unlearn habits that are counterproductive with Serverless.

Many organizations do not hire junior developers (with less than a year of experience building software as a primary job) because they believe, often rightly, that junior developers will not be able to build effectively and will also generate an excess of defects, not to mention drain time from more senior developers. The massive complexity of a typical enterprise codebase is not conducive to bringing in developers who have not worked with something similar in scope. This is a self-perpetuating cycle, and it means that most companies are competing (and driving up salaries) for a much smaller pool of developers than exists.

A well-built Serverless application has less code and much less back-end complexity than a comparable non-Serverless application. Not only does this make the application easier to maintain, but it also makes training new developers easier. The application also generally is harder to break, in surprising ways that are hard to automatically test. This is not to say that an organization can simply turn junior developers loose without oversight on a Serverless codebase; rather, it is possible to hire mostly junior developers and train them successfully on a Serverless application in a way that is not possible with a traditional application architecture. Branch is proof of this; the organization hires almost exclusively junior front-end software developers from the very beginning.

In addition to making it easier to hire junior developers, Serverless applications are generally much easier to do full-stack development on. Until Serverless, the concept of a full-stack developer was more mythical than real, given all the technologies needed to really develop on the entire stack: front-end development, including CSS; API design; back-end development (in a different language than the front end); database design and optimization; and infrastructure as code.

Serverless architectures are so managed-service heavy that the documentation and available training for the vast majority of back-end functionality is quite easy to learn. Managed services also often have excellent developer advocates who provide examples and help for developers at all experience levels to use them. Additionally, it is increasingly common to use JavaScript (or TypeScript) for both the front and back ends of Serverless applications, which has many benefits in turning front-end developers into full-stack developers: less to learn, monorepos, and more code that can be reused without modification.

Even if an organization decides to use several different languages across its application infrastructure, and even if it wants to keep specialization within front- and back-end teams, the benefit of having less code and a simpler deployment framework meaningfully reduces the effort to become a full-stack developer.

Summary: Retraining the Workforce

An organization that is making the shift to Serverless architectures from traditional architectures and intentionally handing off to managed-service providers responsibilities that have been handled internally needs to have a plan to retrain its workforce. Charity Majors's discussion of the new ops jobs is a great read for anyone thinking through operational needs change as applications leverage more managed services.

Any organization rolling out significant changes in how it does things will need to bring most (and, ideally, all) of its people along with it. By identifying opportunities for training alongside a common conversation about how new technologies will enable more efficient software development, organizations can go far together.

References

[1] "The Future of Ops Jobs." https://acloudguru.com/blog/engineering/the-future-of-ops-jobs

[2] www.honeycomb.io/

[3] Debrie, Alex. *The DynamoDB Book.* www.dynamodbbook.com/

Chapter 11

Your Serverless Journey

Now you should understand the Serverless mindset: what it is, how it works technically, what advantages it delivers to organizations, and how to plan its adoption. The most important next step is for you to start on your Serverless journey. This chapter summarizes why Serverless will be a game changer for you and gives specific advice about the first steps to take for different people in different roles in different types of organizations.

Serverless As a Game Changer

An organization's ability to leverage technology effectively is increasingly the key strategic differentiator between failure and success. Successful companies, both startups and industry stalwarts, must continuously pursue new growth opportunities and adapt to a changing world. They must solve unknown, complex problems that are not well understood and, therefore, are even harder to solve. Thus, the most successful organizations can iterate quickly around problem definitions to identify potential solutions. Then by building and releasing technology quickly, these organizations shorten the feedback cycle and innovate at a faster rate based upon market feedback.

The best way to set up an organization for success is to optimize the way the organization uses technology: culture, teams, stack, architecture, and development processes. The best optimization today is to adopt the Serverless mindset: The organization should focus all its efforts on building technology in-house only if it provides a differentiated advantage in the marketplace, and not building anything else. This is because building undifferentiated technology takes time, money, and cognitive capacity, and it almost always ends with a result that is more expensive (in terms of total cost of ownership) and not as good (in terms of user experience and how well it solves the problem) as it could be. Organizations that take a "code is a liability" approach will be more effective at building and releasing technology quickly and iterating rapidly.

When an organization decides that it needs to write custom software to differentiate itself, it should build those applications with Serverless architectures. Serverless architectures delegate all aspects of provisioning and uptime to cloud providers (for example, running on Serverless services at Amazon Web Services) and then delegate significant feature functionality to service providers (for example, using Algolia for searching or Cloudinary for image manipulation). Serverless architectures are the optimal tech stacks for focusing an organization's software development on differentiated innovation that delivers bottom-line impact.

Serverless Steps in Startups

Startups are uniquely qualified to leverage the Serverless mindset and Serverless architectures because they are resource constrained, they are time constrained, and they have no pre-existing teams or technology that must be maintained. Yet frequently, startups choose tech stacks either by choosing a technical cofounder who will be a player/coach in the initial development or by outsourcing software development. The organizations then allow those developers to make the stack selection. Usually, the stack is chosen by whatever the developers have most recently used, and often there is internal discussion that this is "just for the MVP," with an expectation that it will be easy to rewrite in some other stack later, if necessary.

Unfortunately, it is rarely easy to rewrite software, and in order to survive, most startups need to keep consistently shipping features for many years into their existence. Thus, many of the technical choices made early in a startup's existence can have enormous consequences for both the short- and long-term success of the company. Every additional cycle of iteration that a startup can deliver into market decreases the risk that the startup will fail to reach product-market fit; poor choices in tech stack can lead to orders of magnitude fewer cycles per year. Beware the "just for the MVP" mentality: Most teams would never choose to develop a prototype or MVP if they had known it would lead to unchangeable decisions that they made too early.

This section focuses on how different people occupying different positions within a startup can help the startup make good technology choices and mitigate the risks of failure.

Nontechnical Founder

Many nontechnical founders in startups are a bit afraid to wade into discussions of technical choices being made for the organization by a technical founder, lead developer, or outsourced development firm. This is not surprising; it is hard to know how to ask the right questions—or even whether it's appropriate to question at all, given the almost magical output that can come out of the software development process. Software development is not magic, though, and competent oversight even from nontechnical leaders can make an enormous difference in whether the technical departments make the right choices for the organization.

As a nontechnical founder, you must make sure you know how your organization is going to differentiate itself, and you should communicate that to everyone who is going to build software for your organization. You should read *Accelerate* (mentioned previously in Chapter 8, "Getting to Serverless") with your technical leadership and discuss using the metrics detailed in that book in your organization. Some startup technical founders argue that building to these metrics is inappropriate for startups that are just building prototypes; you should not accept that answer. These metrics help developers build *anything* faster and more effectively, including prototypes.

You should understand what your technical teams are spending time working on, and you should be able to connect this directly to key initiatives. You should make sure that your organization is a safe place to do research to find services to buy instead of immediately encouraging developers to build things. Finally, you should set an example of accepting downscoped, imperfect v1s so that your organization does not make *perfect* the enemy of *done*.

Technical Founder

As the technical founder of a startup, it is important to mitigate the many risks of failure, accidental complexity, and decisions made too early. It is well worth spending significant time with other founders to understand how the organization will succeed. Usually this involves significant nontechnical elements, but understanding those will make you a much more effective technical leader. You want to be able to know and anticipate as many business decisions as possible, and you want to avoid being surprised by comments and feedback from other leaders in the organization.

At early stages, startup leaders are making a lot of guesses that will turn out to be incorrect. You do not want to encode all these guesses into technical choices that will be difficult to change later. One of the best ways to avoid making incorrect technical choices is to build Serverlessly: Use managed services, use SaaS for internal functions, and try to focus most custom coding on customer-facing interfaces and business logic. Choosing to use Kubernetes is almost always a bad decision in a startup. So is making any selection that requires having full-time operations staff from the beginning. A startup should be able to leverage its founding technical staff for any on-call rotation if it builds Serverless applications.

Founding Engineer

As the founding engineer of a startup, you might not have as many decisions to make regarding the technical stack or overall architecture as a technical founder, but your decisions will likely have a significant impact on development velocity. It will fall to you to research whether you can use services or libraries instead of writing code. Your recommendation will often be the most important one—and sometimes the only one—in terms of what you will build and what you will buy. If you figure out how you can use an excellent managed service, even if it doesn't have any examples of your specific use case, that will be an enormous help to your organization. If you instead argue for building something in-house because you prefer to build and you don't want to experiment with a service, you could be putting another nail in the coffin of your organization's untimely demise.

You also want to understand enough about how much it costs to pay you and build software in-house so that you can help other leaders in your organization understand that it could be much cheaper to spend $1,000 per month on a service than to build it in-house. Many startups shy away from spending anything but pennies on services to start, oddly valuing cash spent on employees and contractors as somehow less than cash charged monthly by a service. You can help them understand the wisdom and value of limiting what software is developed in-house.

A final warning is specific to Serverless development in startups: Do not start on a path that will lead to hundreds or thousands of Serverless functions that are around 100 lines of code each. This Serverless structure is an anti-pattern, and it will lead to unnecessary complexity and slowness in development velocity. Splitting up larger functions later is much easier than reassembling tight control flow from distributed functions.

Serverless Steps in Small or Medium-Size Organizations

Small and medium-size businesses (SMBs) usually have constrained budgets and existing, functional technology. The potential rate of change within an SMB is much slower than in a startup, and cost savings are often more a driver of change than delivering new or better functionality. In this environment, the most important first focus is building the organization's ability to make changes efficiently and safely. Once software releases happen multiple times per week and automated testing prevents significant bugs from getting into production, the organization will be able to make effective changes at low cost.

Nontechnical Executive

As a nontechnical executive in an SMB, you should make sure your technical teams understand how to value their time and empower them to spend money where it will significantly free up their time. Read *Accelerate*, and understand the metrics that you should hold your technology teams accountable for meeting. Avoid metrics that ultimately lead to worse results, such as lines of code added to the codebase.

Spend enough time with your technical leadership and technology team discussing the organizational focus so that everyone who is building for the organization understands the goals. Developers who have an independent, correct alignment with how you think about priorities will make much better decisions than those who are reliant upon a "telephone" game up through the organization.

Product Management

As a product manager in an SMB, you have significant control over how product features are scoped and assigned. You should also read *Accelerate*, and you should aggressively seek to downscope work, making sure that releases are as frequent as possible. Run retros regularly, and work to adjust your processes so that developers can leverage the velocity benefits of Serverless architectures.

Development Team

As a member of the software development team in an SMB, whether a CTO or an entry-level developer, you will have ample opportunity to identify situations for using managed services instead of custom code. Because so many managed services charge only based on use and often have free tiers, you can perhaps bring significant new value to the organization by taking an hour to hook up a new service (for example, Amazon Cognito, a service that handles user authentication, is free for up to 50,000 users, which could be more than an SMB ever has).

The most difficult part about driving change in an SMB as a member of the technical team is the lack of resources. Limited resources also means that it can be very difficult to allocate time to rebuilding anything that isn't hopelessly, painfully broken. However, good technical leaders figure out how to allocate the needed time and energy to refactoring and rearchitecting. One good strategy is to make sure that every product feature that involves more than a few days of work and touches code that needs some refactoring has that refactoring attached to the development work.

Serverless Steps in the Enterprise for Executives

Large enterprises face different challenges in adopting Serverless than either startups or SMBs. Enterprises have many existing teams and systems that are necessary for keeping the day-to-day operations going. Enterprises can have significant resources to make changes, but only if they are a part of key executive initiatives. Thus, Serverless adoption in enterprises depends entirely upon changing culture and helping people understand why Serverless delivers such significant benefits. This is true for everyone, from executive sponsors down to anyone who will be called upon to implement the changes.

As an executive in a large enterprise, whether technical or nontechnical, you should start by estimating the business impact of making the changes discussed in this book in your area of the business. You can assess the different costs throughout the enterprise that are connected to the current way your organization builds and runs software. You can estimate the gap in agility that your organization has with its current software development lifecycle and what would be possible if your organization operated more like the best teams described in *Accelerate*.

If you do these assessments and see how moving to Serverless would have a significant business impact, you should help all those around you understand what you have found. Think about the cultural and other organizational obstacles that need to be overcome to drive the adoption of Serverless in your organization. You might find that you need some key new personnel in-house or as contractors to help make the right architectural choices. Ultimately, a successful shift to Serverless in an enterprise comes down to leading cultural and technical change.

Serverless Is the Ultimate Step

Now that you understand the benefits of Serverless and have some ideas on how to start building Serverlessly, you might ask, "Is Serverless best seen as an iterative improvement on best-practices cloud development instead of a sea change?"

The answer is, no. Although it's possible to see Serverless architectures as just another step in using cloud infrastructure and cloud service providers, it is also the last step. Once the entire responsibility for infrastructure uptime has been handed off, nothing more *can* be delegated. We should expect that more services will be created and the developer experience will continue to improve, but the general concept of building software by writing business-specific logic on top of managed services will remain the same.

You might also ask, "If we make significant changes to adopt Serverless now, will we be faced with yet another big improvement in software development that requires us to change everything all over again in the future?"

The answer to this question is, the only way to adopt new improvements in software development efficiently is to have the Serverless mindset. Once an organization is focused on spending its efforts only in building differentiation through custom business logic, not in building anything that can be handled by a third-party managed service, no further optimization in philosophy is possible. The only improvements over any given implementation will be in the adoption of new services that enable a sharper focus on what makes the organization special, jettisoning a focus on undifferentiated heavy lifting.

When you see that building Serverlessly is the ultimate way to build software effectively and efficiently, you will also see that the core skill to keep sharp is the ability to adopt new services when they are built. The key cultural belief to instill in your teams is that they should have no aversion to throwing away work on which they have spent significant time. Additionally, they should take pride in how focused they are on building software that delivers the most value to their customers.

Appendix A

Directory: API Hubs

When building a Serverless application, the architectural choice that will drive the most benefits is choosing a managed service as an API Hub. To some extent, the API Hub is the Serverless realization of what Platforms-as-a-Service (PaaS) and Back-ends-as-a-Service (BaaS) previously implemented in a less effective way, but they drive significantly different application architectures and better efficiencies. This appendix explains what an API Hub is and provides several options for API Hub choices for modern Serverless applications.

What Is an API Hub?

An API Hub is a managed service that handles traffic from front-end applications (such as mobile apps and single-page web applications) calling key application functionality, such as authentication and custom back-end code, through managed services. The API Hub is a replacement for running a web server, so any application that includes running Nginx, Express, Passenger, or WEBrick is not leveraging an API Hub. For applications that have different behavior based on authenticated access, the API Hub integrates tightly with an authentication service so that calls to custom back-end code are coupled with identity and access management information to enable much simpler secure access.

This book uses the term *API Hub* because there must necessarily be an application programming interface (API) between front ends and back ends, and the choice of how that API will work can drive either a lot of unnecessary additional work or substantial efficiency in how the entire application can be developed. Better choices in an API Hub can make it the central, driving definition of the core schema of the application and dramatically streamline changes over time.

For example, many modern applications without a central schema require multiple schema changes as data moves from the datastore to the back end (for example, ORM), to the API-defined schema (usually through custom code), to the front end (again, often through custom code). Even more transformations can happen, as with Backend for Frontend (BFF).[1] In these architectures, a separate team usually handles each step, meaning that any change that requires a schema change throughout the application requires coordinating at least three teams; it's extremely unlikely that an individual developer would be able to submit a pull request to do something like add a single new field to an existing form in the front end.

However, to the extent that an application can use the schema within the API Hub to also be the core schema throughout the front end, the back end, and the datastore (e.g., by having a GraphQL schema within the API Hub and storing within a document or key-value store), individual developers significantly increase their chances of being able to work across the entire application. (This gets even easier if the entire application, both front end and back end, is written in the same language and can share the same custom libraries). With an API Hub that has a centralized schema, an individual developer commonly can write all the code needed across the entire stack.

Using an API Hub and a centralized schema is not a silver bullet. Adopting it blindly won't magically make all software developers full-stack developers or definitively make software development much faster. Additionally, there are advantages to data transformation (including enhanced validation and easier handling of joins) that need to be implemented separately with a centralized schema that isn't meaningfully transformed.

Additionally, how many API Hubs an organization should run can be a difficult enterprise architecture question. Branch runs two API Hubs: one for customer-facing interfaces and one for internal- and independent agent–facing interfaces. For Branch, it makes sense to separate these concerns because they have separate sets of authenticated users. A time might come when Branch splits one or more of these API Hubs to reduce interdependence between development teams; it generally makes sense to monolithically deploy the API Hubs.

However, when done properly, using the API Hub with a centralized schema is a better and more efficient way to build applications than building with multiple schemas and transformations. This approach makes it possible to have full-stack developers and also significantly decreases the complexity of applications by eliminating a large amount of code and operational overhead.

API Hub Directory

The rest of this appendix is a directory of API Hub managed services. The primary requirements to be on this list are: (a) An untrusted client application must be able to connect directly to the service and authenticate without writing an intermediary back-end web service, (b) the service must have a database for which access rights can be defined on a per-user and/or per-access group basis, and (c) the service must have a way to run custom back-end code (functions) that has access to both the identity and access management information, as well as the database. Note that, in some cases, the API Hub will use multiple services; in almost all cases, it will offer significant additional, unique functionality.

It is worth noting that plenty of companies are developing Serverless applications that do not use API Hubs. Common architectural choices for them are using API Gateway + Lambda from Amazon Web Services, Cloud Run on Google Cloud, or Static Web Apps + Functions on Azure. There are newer companies as well, especially in the Cloud Run space, such as Railway and Render; it is also perfectly fine to access a database directly from an insecure front end—this can be done securely and is discussed in more detail in Appendix C, "Directory: Databases."

Alternatives to API Hubs are not bad architectures, but they do not achieve the same amount of leverage of developer time and talent that the API Hubs do. Still, any organization building Serverlessly is likely operating more efficiently than organizations using traditional architectures.

AWS AppSync/Amplify

AWS AppSync,[2] usually leveraged as part of AWS Amplify, is a GraphQL API as Service that allows companies to define a GraphQL schema of data structures and function calls and then manages, with the help of other AWS services, the back-end API for an application. AppSync natively uses Cognito for authentication, DynamoDB for a datastore, and Lambda for custom back-end code (see Figure A.1). With AppSync, organizations can easily use other databases and other authentication services if its native choices are not preferable. AppSync uses the Apache Velocity Template Language (VTL) for defining flows between AppSync and AWS services, although, in practice, it is common to send most or all of the AppSync GraphQL requests through custom AWS Lambda functions (in those cases, the VTL necessary is trivial).

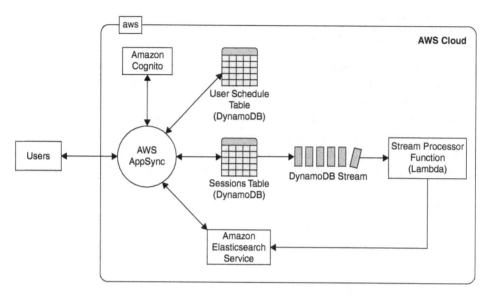

Figure A.1 *Example AppSync Architecture from Amazon Web Services*

AppSync has a number of unique features that are especially useful for mobile app developers (especially when used within the Amplify ecosystem). The most notable of these is Amplify Datastore, which, when used with the Amplify libraries, makes it simple to synchronize data (which is often offline) between an app and the centralized datastore at AWS.

Pros

- Offers the most full-featured API Hub option
- Directly integrates with many AWS services and, through Lambda, to all others
- Boasts excellent historical uptime and stability (GA 4/2018)
- Provides GraphQL schema and support, for significant efficiency benefits
- Works with most major programming languages through Lambda
- Integrates with Amplify for a simpler developer experience
- Low cost

Cons

- The start-up time and learning curve are significantly higher than with other options, and the developer experience is relatively worse.
- Cognito has historically been a low-feature, low-development-velocity authentication service compared to competitors (although it is very reliable).
- Relational database support through Serverless Aurora is not as good as with other RDBMS options.
- Elasticsearch is not Serverless and is generally a weaker alternative than Algolia, which is more tightly integrated in other options (Algolia can be used with AppSync, but it involves more work).
- Because so many services are involved and AWS billing around Serverless services is hard to estimate, bills can be confusing and surprising (although generally not expensive).

Some Companies Using AppSync in Production[3]

- Branch
- State Auto
- Peacock (Comcast)
- Aldo
- Neiman Marcus

Pricing

AppSync's pricing is inexpensive, relative to the other AWS services that will be used as part of the overall application architecture. Branch's June 2022 AWS bill was around $10,000, of which $42.09 was for AppSync. The top five services that Branch paid for in that bill were DynamoDB (about $4,000), Lambda ($2,200), CloudWatch ($1,000), CloudTrail ($600), and S3 ($300).

Recommended Resources

- Amazon: https://aws.amazon.com/appsync/
- AppSync Masterclass: https://appsyncmasterclass.com/
- *Full Stack Serverless*, by Nader Dabit (book)

Google Firebase[4]

Firebase was founded in 2011 as one of the original API Hubs (called Backends as a Service at the time). Google purchased it in 2014 and has continued to build it out, most notably in adding Firestore as an option and also adding functions support.

Firebase is a collection of specific Firebase services, along with a platform that enables easier use of other services that are tied together in a console, APIs, and a command-line interface (see Figure A.2). Firebase runs a RESTful API, along with libraries in many languages that make using the API very easy; it handles identity and access management, calls to back-end functions, and data reads/writes from its datastores. Firebase offers two datastores: the real-time database, which is best for applications that need to synchronize state between clients quickly, and Firestore, a MongoDB-like document datastore that is probably the best choice for all other uses.

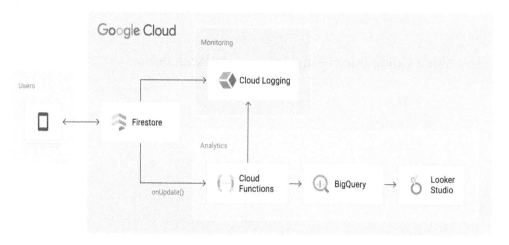

Figure A.2 *Example Firebase Architecture from Google*

A simplistic way to think about Firebase is that it is less full featured but is much easier to use, with a much better developer experience (DX) compared to AWS AppSync.

Pros

- Provides the most tightly integrated set of services for any API Hub
- Offers the best developer experience of any API Hub
- Directly integrates with many Google Cloud services and, through cloud functions, to all others

- Also directly integrates tightly with several external services, including a Firestore/Algolia integration that makes searching data easy and secure
- Boasts excellent historical uptime and stability
- Works with most major programming languages through cloud functions

Cons

- Not as many services and not as full featured as the AWS ecosystem
- Complex security rules system for access management
- No native GraphQL or centralized schema support
- Potentially expensive at very large database sizes or large data transfer amounts

Some Companies Using Firebase in Production

- NPR
- Instacart
- LaunchDarkly

Pricing

Somewhat like AWS, Firebase bases pricing on the use of individual Firebase and Google Cloud services. Firebase has a generous free tier, but it can be quite expensive at larger sizes. For example, the real-time database (at the time of publication) was billed at $5 per GB-month, measuring both storage and data transfer.

Recommended Resources

- Google: https://firebase.google.com/
- Udemy course: www.udemy.com/course/firebase-course/

Fauna[5]/(Netlify[6] or Vercel[7])/Auth0

The longest-standing alternative to a major cloud provider service is Fauna, a Serverless document database, used in combination with one of the best two front-end hosting and function running services, either Netlify or Vercel. All of these services have a great track record: Fauna has been around since 2012, Netlify since 2014, and Vercel since 2015.

Fauna is both a GraphQL Serverless database and an authentication service that can use the database for access management. This Fauna + static hosting stack is the simplest way to build a full-fledged Serverless application, and it can be thought of as an enhanced JAMstack (JavaScript, API, and Markup). With JAMstack, the bulk of the application logic lives in the front end, although both Netlify and Vercel run Serverless cloud functions that can run protected back-end code (see Figure A.3).

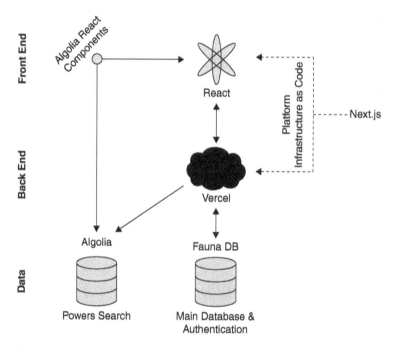

Figure A.3 *Example FaunaDB + Vercel Architecture from Mike Rispoli*

Many people choose to use Auth0 as their identity and access management service alongside Fauna and either Netlify or Vercel because Auth0's service is more full-featured than Fauna's native authentication service.

Pros

- Architecturally simpler than AWS AppSync or Google Firebase
- Native support for push to GitHub and deploy

- Native support for branch deploys while testing at little additional cost
- Fast deployments
- Native support for server-side rendering (SSR)
- Excellent support for complex queries

Cons

- Much more limited than AWS or Google ecosystems in terms of additional native services
- Steeper learning curve for Fauna than Firebase, especially with the Fauna Query Language (FQL) for more complicated queries
- Fairly simplistic identity and access management, often leading people to seek out an alternative such as Auth0
- Not great for applications with significant amounts of back-end logic
- More limited language support for functions (usually just JavaScript or TypeScript)

Some Companies Using Netlify or Vercel in Production

- Peloton
- Nike
- Netflix
- eBay

Pricing

Because this API Hub option uses multiple services from different providers, cost almost certainly will be higher than with other options. Fauna charges per use at a cost not dissimilar to DynamoDB. Netlify and Vercel charge per developer; with a small development team, the prices are fairly low, but expect to pay a significant amount for a significant number of developers. Auth0 prices per user, so it can be cost-prohibitive for an application with a large number of users.

Recommended Resources

- Fauna: www.fauna.com

- Netlify: www.netlify.com

- Vercel: www.vercel.com

- Auth0: www.auth0.com

- Simple Egghead course: https://egghead.io/courses/building-a-serverless-jam-stack-todo-app-with-netlify-gatsby-graphql-and-faunadb-53bb

- More complex Egghead course: https://egghead.io/courses/full-stack-serverless-applications-with-next-js-fauna-35bd6879

- Simple tutorial: https://dev.to/mrispoli24/building-a-serverless-stack-overflow-for-students-learning-at-home-38in

- Fauna/Netlify integration: https://docs.fauna.com/fauna/current/build/integrations/netlify

- Fauna/Vercel Integration: https://vercel.com/integrations/fauna

Supabase[8]

This API Hub option is based upon much newer services than any of the others mentioned in this appendix. Supabase markets itself as an open-source Firebase alternative. It is open source and is built from open source software, but it also offers a hosted solution. It is not a replica of Firebase, but rather is generally a feature match to what Firebase offers.

The Supabase database is PostgreSQL, its identity and access management integrate directly with PostgreSQL for row-level access, and it allows access from front-end applications using RESTful, real-time, and GraphQL APIs. See Figure A.4 for Supabase's architecture, including how it also hosts and runs functions and has an object storage repository.

Pros

- The only relational database–based API Hub option

- The most fully integrated API Hub option

- Tight integration support with services such as Auth0 and Vercel

- Underlying open-source code, which might appeal to some customers

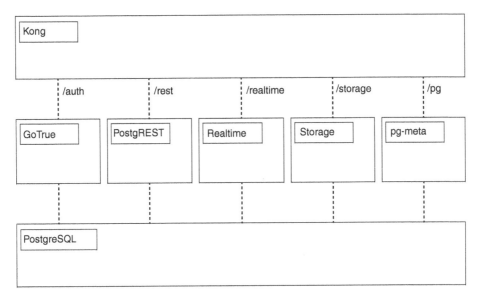

Figure A.4 *Supabase Open-Source Architecture*

Cons

- Much more limited than AWS or Google ecosystems in terms of additional native services, especially for telephony and mobile apps
- Relatively new and unproven (as of publication)
- Limited language support for functions

Pricing

Supabase pricing is based on metered usage. An enterprise level of pricing is also offered but not disclosed.

Recommended Resources

- Supabase: www.supabase.com/
- Udemy course: www.udemy.com/course/supabase-from-scratch-serverless-database-backend-with-javascript/

References

[1] https://learn.microsoft.com/en-us/azure/architecture/patterns/backends-for-frontends

[2] https://aws.amazon.com/appsync/

[3] https://aws.amazon.com/appsync/customers/

[4] https://firebase.google.com/

[5] https://fauna.com/

[6] www.netlify.com/

[7] https://vercel.com/

[8] https://supabase.com/

Appendix B

Directory: Identity and Access Management

Most commercial applications have significant human identity and access management (IAM) requirements. There are security requirements (such as multifactor authentication, the need to conceal which email addresses correspond to accounts, and the need to force lockouts after a certain number of failures), usability requirements (such as password resets, social login, and login by phone), and enterprise integration requirements (such as single sign-on or use of a corporate identity provider). Thus, it rarely makes sense to build that system from scratch or even to use a library—using a managed service is usually much better.

What Does an IAM Managed Service Do?

IAM services handle verifying users' identities and providing that verification alongside access details to custom code and other managed services to manage what features and information the user is entitled to use and see. IAM services manage many different ways of authenticating users, from username/password combinations, to one-time-passwords via email or SMS, to social logins, to SAML integrations with corporate identity platforms. IAM services also provide easy ways to handle signups, email address and phone number verifications, password resets, and other account management needs.

IAM Directory

The rest of this appendix is a directory of IAM managed services. The primary requirements to be on this list are that the provider is serverless, provides a datastore for users and some associated metadata, and allows for some method of differentiated access management.

The providers in this appendix are listed in the order in which they launched. All have been around for a significant period of time and have proven their stability. Newer startups in the IAM space have not gone after their entire feature sets, perhaps because these solutions are good enough and they do not see enough reason to compete directly with them. Instead, new entrants tend to be add-ons to enable passwordless/additional methods of login (as with Stytch); full enterprise security requirements (as with WorkOS); or open-source projects that are designed to be self-hosted and, even in hosted form, are not serverless (as with FusionAuth and Ory).

Google Firebase Authentication[1]

Firebase Authentication was launched alongside Firebase (now called the "real-time database") in 2012. It was an integral part of the original Firebase product, allowing untrusted, front-end applications to communicate directly with the Firebase service to handle the authenticated retrieval of information based on specific rules set up in Firebase configuration (see Figure B.1). After Firebase's acquisition by Google, the Firebase team continued to enhance Firebase authentication, adding many identity provider plug-ins (including Google, social media logins, SAML, and OAuth 2.0), as well as multifactor authentication and enhanced rules syntax to provide user- and role-based access.

Firebase Authentication can be used without Firebase, although doing so likely does not make much sense because such a significant part of Firebase Authentication's benefit lies in its security rules. Firebase Authentication also integrates closely with Firebase Storage, used for objects and files, as well as Firebase Functions, which execute custom back-end code. Additionally, Firebase Authentication is commonly used to drive centralized authentication for mobile applications, as well as other Google Cloud services, such as App Engine.

Pros

- Great developer experience and documentation
- Excellent integration with other Firebase (and some Google Cloud) services
- Low price

Figure B.1 *Firebase Authentication Security Rules Playground*

Cons

- Not as good a choice outside Firebase or Google Cloud
- Requires the use of Firebase to be a full IAM solution
- Simplistic and limited web console for management

Some Companies Using Firebase Authentication in Production

- Twitch
- Duolingo
- Instacart

Pricing

Firebase includes Firebase Authentication for a significant number of users in its paid Blaze plan. The cost is mostly driven by the amount of data that is in and transferred to and from the Firebase database. At the time of publication, the first 50,000 monthly active users and first 10,000 phone authentications (if using SMS) in the

United States, Canada, or India are provided at no charge. Beyond those, additional users are charged at $0.0055 (less than a penny) per monthly active user or less. Phone authentications are charged at 1 cent (for U.S., Canada, or India) or 5 cents (for other countries) each.

Recommended Resources

- Firebase Authentication: https://firebase.google.com/docs/auth
- Udemy Course: www.udemy.com/course/firebase-authentication/

Auth0[2]

Auth0 was released in 2013 as a standalone identity management service. From day one, Auth0 integrated with many different identity providers (including Active Directory, Google, Office365, OpenLDAP, Twitter, and Facebook) and enabled anyone to make an application authenticate against those providers. Auth0 then expanded into allowing its customers to store more information on each use profile and built a full-featured, web-based console that enabled searching, viewing, and modifying user records (see Figure B.2). Auth0 has continued to add features, especially around serverless architectures, from using JAMstack to being an alternative to cloud-specific identity services.

In 2021, Okta, a provider of single-sign-on identity services for enterprises, acquired Auth0. Okta's original solution can also be an option for human IAM within custom applications, especially if an organization is already using it and just wants to leverage it for administrative authentication. The Auth0 solution is better for customer authentication.

Pros

- Works equally well with all clouds
- Has the widest array of identity provider support
- Has the most full-featured web console of any identity provider
- Provides the best fully integrated IAM solution; others must be used with other cloud services to reach their full potential

Figure B.2 *Auth0 Dashboard*

Cons

- Has a history of breaking changes with new feature releases
- In the past, has had worse uptime than either Firebase Authentication or Amazon Cognito (as of this publication, 99.95% uptime over the past 12 months)
- Costs much more than other options

Some Companies Using Auth0 in Production

- Dick's Sporting Goods
- Kiva
- Toast

Pricing

Auth0 has consistently increased pricing over time, differentiating between use cases to drive prices higher if companies are likely to have fewer users that will pay them more. In Auth0's consumer-facing application pricing, 10,000 monthly active users costs either $228 per month or $1,500 per month, depending on what functionality is needed. For business-facing applications, that range is $1,420 per month to $1,800 per month for only 7,000 users. At volumes above those, prospects need to contact Auth0 directly for custom pricing.

Recommended Resources

- Auth0 documentation: https://auth0.com/docs/
- Udemy has many courses that show how to connect Auth0 to various front-end application frameworks, most of which are good value.

Amazon Cognito[3]

Amazon Cognito was released in 2014 as a service to manage identities, access management, and manage data for mobile applications. In 2014, many mobile app developers were looking for managed services to handle saving relatively small amounts of data in the cloud for their apps. At the time, perhaps the most popular service was Parse (later acquired by Facebook and then shut down), and Cognito was widely viewed as a competitor to Parse.

Today Cognito is recommended for and used by all types of applications, including desktop and web-based applications. Cognito has historically had fantastic performance and uptime but has fewer features than competitors and relatively slow development velocity. Prior to 2022, the Cognito console was almost unusably limited, but the recent updates have been excellent and hopefully signal an era of improved investment in Cognito. See Figure B.3 for an example of how Cognito security integrates into AWS AppSync.

Pros

- Simplest powerful IAM with Amplify and AppSync
- Most affordable identity solution
- Best historical uptime and performance
- Low price

```
# Admin operations
createUniversity(
  name: String!
  profileName: String!
  centerName: String!
  adminEmail: AWSEmail!
  imageUrl: AWSURL!
  location: LocationInput!
  profilePic: AWSURL!
  coverPhoto: AWSURL!
): University
@aws_auth(cognito_groups: ["Admin"])

# University operations
updateMyUniversity(
  imageUrl: AWSURL!
  location: LocationInput!
  profilePic: AWSURL!
  coverPhoto: AWSURL!
): University
@aws_auth(cognito_groups: ["University"])
```

Figure B.3 *How Cognito Manages Authorization Configuration in AppSync*

Cons

- Poor documentation
- Complex options (for example, User Pool vs. Identity Pool)
- More limited user attribute storage (less space, fewer custom attributes)
- Limited user search (can't search by many attributes)

Some Companies Using Cognito in Production

- Branch
- Neiman Marcus
- *The Wall Street Journal*

Pricing

Amazon Cognito's pricing is essentially the same as with Firebase Authentication (although Cognito established this pricing first). The first 50,000 monthly active users are free, and then each additional monthly active user is $0.0055.

Recommended Resources

- Amazon Cognito: https://aws.amazon.com/cognito/
- Udemy course: www.udemy.com/course/amazon-cognito-the-complete-introduction-2019/
- The Case For and Against Cognito: https://theburningmonk.com/2021/03/the-case-for-and-against-amazon-cognito/

References

[1] https://firebase.google.com/docs/auth

[2] https://auth0.com/blog/announcing-auth0/

[3] https://aws.amazon.com/cognito/

Appendix C

Directory: Databases

Almost every commercial software application has a need to save data in a centralized database or datastore. Many different types of databases and interfaces to databases have been built since 2010, and every month seems to bring even more experimentation and innovation. In the very early days of Serverless, the limited availability of Serverless databases meant that database choice was usually the most important and drove other decisions. With the larger number of database options today, it likely makes more sense to start with the choice of API Hub and authentication providers and then select a database that works best with those choices.

What Does a Database Managed Service Do?

A Serverless database managed service creates, updates, and deletes data via requests from front-end (potentially through an API Hub) and back-end applications, restricting access only to authorized users. A Serverless database should scale infinitely (or at least to very high volumes) without its customers needing to do anything. A Serverless database can use standard SQL, GraphQL, or an arbitrary API. Ideally, it should have library support for popular languages, including integration with at least one IAM service so that security does not require significant custom coding.

Database Directory

The rest of this appendix is a directory of database managed services. The primary requirements to be on this list are that the database is rated for production workloads, is Serverless, and can be accessed from an untrusted front-end application or mobile app without requiring any private networks, virtual machines, or containers to be run. Additionally, the provider should charge based upon usage only, and the service provider must oversee all failover and uptime operations. The databases listed here are primary transactional/operational databases, not analytical databases, because those are the databases most generally used by custom-built software.

Many databases that advertise themselves as Serverless do not meet the criteria therein. For example, Supabase isn't purely usage-based pricing, doesn't scale to zero or automatically scale up, and has significant direct connection limitations. Serverless Aurora v1 must be run within an AWS virtual private cloud (VPC). Serverless Aurora v2 doesn't have usage-based billing or API-based querying. MongoDB Atlas isn't rated for production workloads.

AWS DynamoDB

DynamoDB is a key-value store originally built by Amazon to handle massive traffic for its consumer retail operations in the mid-2000s.[1] Amazon Web Services launched its version of the service in 2012 and has made it more feature rich and more Serverless over the more than ten years it has been available (originally, it required buying dedicated capacity). On Amazon Prime Day 2022, DynamoDB handled trillions of calls, peaking at 105.2 million requests per second, with single-digit-millisecond response times.[2] See Figure C.1 for an example of how DynamoDB stores data.

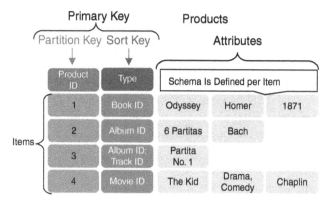

Figure C.1 *Example DynamoDB Table*

Pros

- Fast, reliable, and consistent performance
- The most popular and widely used Serverless database
- Native integration with AWS Amplify and AppSync
- DynamoDB Streams that enable easy event-based processing of changes at scale, for ETL or other use cases

Cons

- Slow non-key-based queries (scans), and analytical analysis and full-text searching needs to be done on a copy of the data in another database (such as AWS Redshift or Snowflake)
- No JOIN support—must be done in custom code
- Requirement for migrations to be done in custom code, iterating over all records
- Need to run additional AWS services—not a standalone Serverless database that works directly with other clouds

Some Companies Using DynamoDB in Production

- Branch
- Amazon.com
- Zoom
- Snap

Pricing

DynamoDB has two modes: on-demand capacity, which autoscales from zero to as much as an application needs; and provisioned capacity, which provides lower costs for more consistent, dedicated traffic. In both cases, pricing is based on (a) the read and write volume to DynamoDB, where the read volume is priced at roughly one-fifth of the write volume, (b) the amount of data stored, which is priced at $0.25 per GB-month (with the first 25GB-month free), and (c) backups, which are priced at $0.20 cents per GB-month for point-in-time recovery going back 35 days and $0.10 cents per GB-month for managed backup storage. As of June 2022, Branch spends significantly more on backups (about $2,500 per month) than reads, writes, and online storage combined (about $1,500 per month), with hundreds of thousands of daily transactions.

Recommended Resources

- *The DynamoDB Book*: www.dynamodbbook.com/
- Dynobase: https://dynobase.dev/
- Coursera course: www.coursera.org/learn/dynamodb-nosql-database-driven-apps

Google Firebase and Firestore

Google Firebase, now called the real-time database, was originally created as a Serverless database for real-time communications between multiple web or mobile applications. It stores data essentially as a single JSON file, with support for a maximum depth of 32 levels. After Google acquired Firebase, it launched Google Firestore, which is more of a MongoDB-style database that has collections, each of which contains documents, each of which can contain subcollections, and on down for 100 levels. Google recommends the real-time database for uses that require real-time communications; Firestore is recommended for everything else. See Figure C.2 for an example of a Firestore collection.

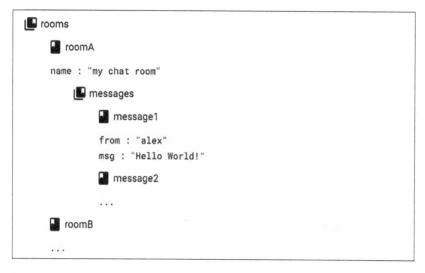

Figure C.2 *Google Firestore Data Model Example*

Pros

- Excellent documentation and developer experience
- Designed to interact directly with front-end applications, with no additional services or custom back-end coding needed
- Firestore relational model and searching capabilities make implementing advanced functionality easier than with DynamoDB[3]
- Good library support for several popular languages and frameworks

Cons

- Querying capabilities are still not as robust as databases that support SQL.
- Migrations must be done in custom code, iterating over all records.
- Full-text searching requires use of Algolia, but the integration works very well.
- The maximum sustained write volume is 1 write per second.

Some Companies Using Firebase in Production

- NPR
- Instacart
- Launch Darkly

Pricing

At the time of publication, the real-time database is billed at $5 per GB-month, measuring both storage and data transfer. Firestore is billed at $0.108 per gibibyte (GiB) over the first GiB, with the first 20,000 writes per day, the first 50,000 reads per day, and the first 10 GiB per month transfer included. At larger volumes of transactions, Firestore tends to be more expensive than DynamoDB, although both are very affordable when compared with non-Serverless options.

Recommended Resources

- Google documentation: https://firebase.google.com/docs/guides
- Firefoo: https://firefoo.app/

Microsoft Azure Cosmos DB

CosmosDB, originally launched in 2017, was created to be the NoSQL database for the Azure cloud. Since then, it has added substantial additional features, enabling it to be used Serverlessly and also queried via many different methods, including SQL and a MongoDB-compatible API (see Figure C.3). Cosmos DB indexes fields for fast query performance without preplanning and has built-in support for graph data and geospatial data.

CosmosDB is the best Serverless datastore option on Azure. It can be combined with Azure Functions, Azure Static Web Apps, and Azure Active Directory to be a Serverless application stack. To the extent that storing all users in Active Directory is a viable application authentication solution (which it usually isn't outside internal applications because of the awkwardness of having end users within the domain), Cosmos DB can run role-based access control to specific data within the database.

Pros

- Unparalleled options for the type of data stored and the capability to query it among Serverless databases

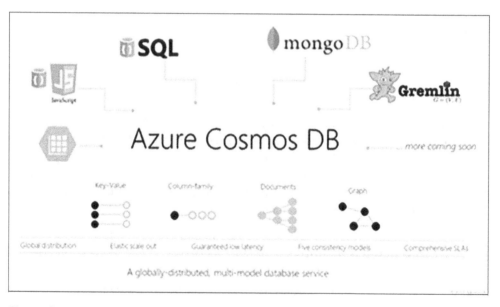

Figure C.3 *The Many Datastores and Query Engines of Cosmos DB*

- Tight integration with other Azure services
- Powerful backup options, including a continuous mode that enables restoration to any point in the past 30 days
- Excellent historical availability and low latency

Cons

- Not nearly as useful outside the Azure cloud as within it
- Fine-grained access control requires Active Directory
- Somewhat limited supported SQL—for example, no JOIN support and no support for GROUP BY
- A hard logical partition maximum size of 20GB, making partition key selection very important

Some Companies Using Cosmos DB in Production

- Albertson's
- DHL
- ExxonMobil

Pricing

Cosmos DB pricing is similar to DynamoDB pricing. Both have a Serverless pricing option and a provisioned throughput option that gives lower pricing in exchange for a dedicated commitment of constant transaction volume support.[4] As with DynamoDB, Cosmos DB has its own proprietary notion of "units" that support a particular amount of transaction volume from which the price is based, along with the cost of storage and transfer. Also similar to DynamoDB, online storage is $0.25 per GB-month. Head-to-head pricing comparisons tend to find Cosmos DB to be marginally more expensive than DynamoDB.[5]

Recommended Resources

- Microsoft's documentation: https://docs.microsoft.com/en-us/azure/cosmos-db/introduction

- Coursera course: www.coursera.org/learn/microsoft-azure-cosmos-db
- Udemy course: www.udemy.com/course/azure-cosmosdb/

FaunaDB

FaunaDB was built by ex-Twitter engineers to be a multitenant, autoscaling, distributed database. Originally released in 2012, it was designed to provide ACID-compliant transactions within a geographically distributed database and based on the Calvin database paper, with a database/document/collection (similar to MongoDB) data model.[6] FaunaDB was originally written to be queried with a SQL-like syntax called Fauna Query Language (FQL).

In the past decade, FaunaDB has added many additional features, including built-in fine-grained access control, GraphQL-based querying, user-defined functions, and library support for many popular languages. FaunaDB has also built out many integrations with other managed services, which makes it compatible with many different Serverless architectures, including Netlify, Vercel, Appsmith, Cloudflare Works, Fastly Compute@Edge, Retool, and WunderGraph.

Pros

- Established, reliable, performant Serverless database
- Excellent library support for popular languages
- User-defined function support
- Integrated fine-grained access control (see Figure C.4)

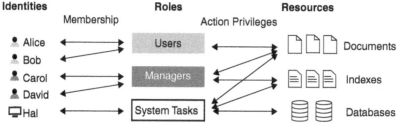

Figure C.4 *Example of FaunaDB Access Control*

Cons

- Function support is much more limited than what is possible within the AWS AppSync or Google Firebase ecosystems.
- FQL is not SQL; it has a learning curve, and lift-and-shift from RDBMS to Fauna is not possible.
- At the time of publication, there is no support in ETL services (such as Fivetran, Stitch Data, or Hevodata) for FaunaDB, so indexing to a data lake is nontrivial.

Some Companies Using FaunaDB in Production

- CapitalOne
- Nvidia
- Nextdoor

Pricing

As with many other Serverless databases, FaunaDB pricing is based upon usage: storage per GB-month (priced at $0.25 per GB-month, per replica), and reads and writes priced per operations ($0.50 per one million reads, and $2.50 per one million writes). Fauna's user-defined functions are provided at additional cost. This means that, by default, Fauna is generally (usually?) more expensive than DynamoDB. However, if workloads are optimized for Fauna, it can be significantly cheaper than DynamoDB.[7]

Recommended Resources

- Fauna tutorials: https://docs.fauna.com/fauna/current/learn/tutorials/
- Egghead courses on Fauna: https://egghead.io/q/faunadb

CockroachDB Serverless

CockroachDB was founded in 2015 by ex-Google employees seeking to build a commercial version of a managed database service similar to Google's Spanner, which is not unlike Calvin/FaunaDB: It is a distributed database that provides ACID-compliant transactions (see Figure C.5). Originally, CockroachDB was offered as a managed service similar to AWS RDS, with allocated VMs or containers of a specific size, or with the option to self-host. Those options still exist, but in 2021, CockroachDB launched its CockroachDB Serverless option, which charges per use and automatically scales.

CockroachDB uses SQL as its query language. Its syntax is most similar to PostgreSQL, but it does not support many special capabilities of PostgreSQL, including stored productions, functions, and user-defined functions; FULLTEXT indexes; PostGIS support; XML functions; and column-level privileges. CockroachDB Serverless replicates all client data in at least three places, scales workloads based on usage, and automatically handles failover and upgrades.

Pros

- Mostly PostgreSQL compatible, including features that are superior to other relational databases (such as PostgreSQL JSON support)

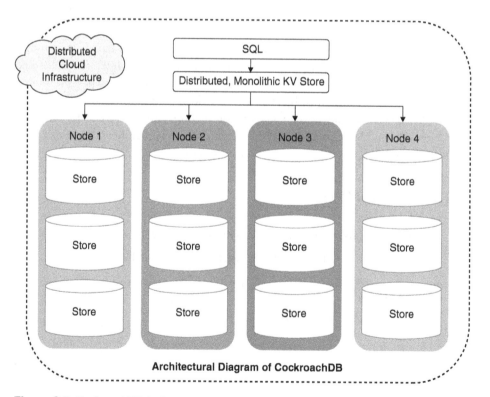

Figure C.5 *CockroachDB Architecture*

- Fast cold starts after being scaled to zero, typically around 600ms
- Currently the best Serverless PostgreSQL-compatible managed database service

Cons

- Does not offer all CockroachDB features in CockroachDB Serverless (including multiregion support)
- Does not support all PostgreSQL features, limiting the ability to lift-and-shift and leverage the unique benefits of PostgreSQL
- Cannot integrate directly with untrusted front ends because it has no direct integrations with authentication providers; requires a service such as Prisma or a custom function
- As of the time of publication, is still in beta

Some Companies Using CockroachDB in Production

- Comcast
- LaunchDarkly
- Shipt

Pricing

CockroachDB pricing is similar to other Serverless database pricing, charging for storage and for simultaneous read/write capacity. As of publication, CockroachDB charges $1 per additional GiB storage (above the 5GiB included in the free plan) and $1 for each additional ten million "request units."

Recommended Resources

- CockroachDB documentation: www.cockroachlabs.com/docs/stable/
- Using CockroachDB with Prisma: www.prisma.io/cockroachdb
- CockroachDB PostgreSQL compatibility: www.cockroachlabs.com/docs/stable/postgresql-compatibility.html

PlanetScale

PlanetScale was founded in 2018 by the creators of the open-source Vitess project, which handles database management, including scaling, for large clusters of MySQL databases (see Figure C.6). Before PlanetScale, managed-service offerings of MySQL had been individual VM or container based, starting with AWS's Relational Database Service (RDS) in 2009. These models require selecting and manually upgrading the underlying hardware specifications, as well as managing a number of different administrative tasks, including upgrading versions of the database and addressing running out of storage.

PlanetScale is a Serverless offering for MySQL, automatically handling all administrative tasks for its customers. Additionally, it has built-in support for separate branch deployments, making it much easier to test database migrations and to run end-to-end tests within both continuous integration workflows and other places in the development life cycle prior to release.

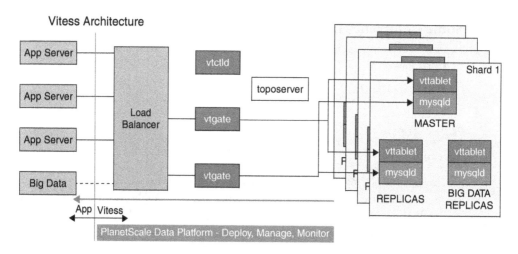

Figure C.6 *PlanetScale's Vitess-Based Architecture*

Pros

- Supports most of MySQL's features (versions 5.7 through 8.0), making lift-and-shift a real possibility for many existing applications
- Offers branch deploys, which can be a huge advantage in developing more efficiently with greater quality assurance
- Best MySQL Serverless managed database service

Cons

- Does not support all MySQL features—most notably, does not support foreign keys, has limited JSON support, and supports only the InnoDB storage engine
- Cannot integrate directly with untrusted front ends because it has no direct integrations with authentication providers; requires a service such as Prisma or custom functions
- Runs only in AWS regions for now and is not natively globally distributed (you select your desired single write region and read regions)

Some Companies Using PlanetScale in Production

- GitHub
- New Relic
- Square

Pricing

PlanetScale pricing is more like enterprise SaaS and developer tools pricing than the other Serverless databases mentioned. PlanetScale has different tiers of service that vary in their amounts of storage, read and write volumes, and branch support, among other features. As of publication, the free tier offers 5GB storage, one billion row reads per month, and ten million row writes per month. The Scaler tier costs $29+ per month and offers 10GB storage, 100 billion row reads per month, and 50 million row writes per month. The Team tier costs $599+ per month and offers 100GB storage, 500 billion row reads per month, and 100 million row writes per month. Enterprise plans start at $2,999 per month.

Recommended Resources

- PlanetScale documentation: https://planetscale.com/docs
- PlanetScale + Prisma + Vercel tutorial: https://davidparks.dev/blog/planetscale-deployment-with-prisma/
- PlanetScale MySQL compatibility: https://planetscale.com/docs/reference/mysql-compatibility

---

Neon and Surreal DB

At the time of publication, two databases were in early development but appear to be interesting new Serverless databases: Neon and Surreal DB.

Neon is a Serverless database service that separates its storage from compute. It is 100% PostgreSQL compatible, which means that, for many Serverless applications, it should be a better option than the other PostgreSQL-like Serverless/Serverless-like database options (such as CockroachDB and Aurora). It remains to be seen how multiregion or global Neon will be, but the initial beta of Neon appears to fill a significant market need.

SurrealDB positions itself as an autoscaling "NewSQL" database, built for accessing from both front-end and back-end code. Additionally, SurrealDB is attempting to handle the storage of tables, documents, and graph-style data, all through a SQL-like language. SurrealDB uses web sockets for client connections and purports to run real-time live queries, as in the Firebase real-time database, but with many additional features.

Depending on how mission-critical the application is, and depending also on the future maturity of these databases, they could be well worth a closer examination.

Links

- Neon: https://neon.tech
- SurrealDB: https://surrealdb.com/

References

[1] DynamoDB Paper. www.allthingsdistributed.com/files/amazon-dynamo-sosp2007.pdf

[2] https://aws.amazon.com/blogs/aws/amazon-prime-day-2022-aws-for-the-win/

[3] https://ezfire.io/blog/cloud-firestore-vs-dynamodb/

[4] https://dynobase.dev/dynamodb-vs-cosmos/

[5] https://acloudguru.com/blog/engineering/comparing-cloud-nosql-databases-dynamodb-vs-cosmos-db-vs-cloud-datastore-and-bigtable

[6] https://fauna.com/blog/distributed-consistency-at-scale-spanner-vs-calvin

[7] https://fauna.com/blog/comparing-fauna-and-dynamodb-pricing-features

Appendix D

Directory: Functions

Although it is possible to write applications that do not require any custom back-end code execution, almost all applications ultimately require running custom functions in a trusted environment. Choices abound for running back-end code as Serverless functions, so this should not be a stumbling block for many architects in designing Serverless applications.

What Does Functions Service Do?

A functions service runs custom code Serverlessly. Developers write code in their own development environment and define the infrastructure around how the code should be executed; once deployed, the service takes responsibility for all running, scaling, failover, and any other operational tasks. For Serverless web applications, the functions service must provide some way for the code to be called from an untrusted front end—ideally, in a way that integrates with an authentication service.

Functions Directory

The rest of this appendix is a directory of services that run custom functions. Unlike the other appendixes in this book, this one does not list every possible Serverless functions service that exists, nor does it go into as much detail for each because most of these services are quite similar. Finding a functions service should be the simplest part of designing a Serverless application; it's important to first define every other part of a Serverless application before looking for which service within the application will be the best provider of a functions service. For example, when designing an application that primarily handles text-message communication, it might make the most sense to use Twilio Functions.

AWS Lambda

Lambda, initially released in 2014, is the functions service that Amazon Web Services runs. It integrates into many other Amazon Web Services, and it has a significant amount of adoption and a large developer community.

Features

- **Longest function runtime:** 15 minutes
- **Largest function size:** 50MB compressed, 250MB uncompressed
- **Maximum memory allocation:** 10,240MB
- **Languages supported natively:** Java, Go, PowerShell, Node.js, C#, Python, Ruby
- **Access from front ends:** API Gateway and AppSync, among others
- **Authentication integration:** Cognito, through API Gateway and AppSync

Pricing

Lambda pricing varies by compute architecture (for example, x86 vs. Arm), based on how much memory the function uses and for how long the function runs (for example, $0.000016667 per GB-second). It also involves a flat amount (currently $0.20) per one million requests.

https://aws.amazon.com/lambda/

Google Functions

Google Functions, generally available starting in 2018, is the functions service that Google Cloud runs. It integrates into many other Google Cloud services, including being wrapped by Firebase as Firebase Functions. Google Functions are widely used, although not as much as AWS Lambda.

Features

- **Longest function runtime:** 9 minutes for 1st gen, 60 minutes for 2nd gen
- **Largest function size:** 100MB compressed, 500MB uncompressed (1st gen), N/A (2nd gen)
- **Maximum memory allocation:** 8GB 1st gen, 16GB 2nd gen
- **Languages supported natively:** Node.js, Python 3, Go, Java, .NET Core, Ruby, PHP
- **Access from front ends:** Native support within Google Cloud Functions
- **Authentication integration:** Firebase Authentication

Pricing

Google Functions pricing is like AWS Lambda pricing: It is based on how much memory the function uses and for how the long the function runs (for example, $0.0000025 per GB-second in Tier1), as well as a flat amount (currently $0.40) per one million requests, above the first two million.

https://cloud.google.com/functions

Azure Functions

Azure Functions is the Microsoft Azure Serverless function platform, originally launched as generally available in 2017. As with Lambda and Google Functions, Azure Functions integrate across Azure's other services and have significant adoption within the Azure and Microsoft development communities. The feature limits here are from the Consumption plan, which is the fully Serverless pricing option.

Features

- **Longest function runtime:** 10 minutes (but 230 seconds when HTTP triggered)
- **Largest function size:** 1GB
- **Maximum memory allocation:** 14GB

- **Languages supported natively:** C#, JavaScript, F#, Java, PowerShell, Python, TypeScript
- **Access from front ends:** Native support within Azure Functions (HTTP Trigger)
- **Authentication integration:** Azure AD, although probably not appropriate for external applications

Pricing

Azure Functions pricing is like AWS Lambda pricing: It is based on how much memory the function uses and for how the long the function runs (for example, $0.000016 per GB-second), along with a flat amount (currently $0.20) per one million requests, above the first one million.

https://docs.microsoft.com/en-us/azure/azure-functions/functions-overview

Netlify Functions

Netlify launched its Serverless functions service in 2018 to provide a way to run custom back-end code alongside front ends deployed through Netlify. Netlify functions were originally backed only by AWS Lambda, but Netlify makes it simpler and easier to develop, package, and deploy the functions into production. More recently, Netlify has expanded where its functions run to include Netlify's own build environment and its own content delivery network. Netlify also acquired Quirrel to add some advanced scheduling and handling of function execution.

Netlify functions make the entire Netlify platform capable of running full-feature applications without having to learn the ins and outs of many services within primary cloud vendors. If an application can fit entirely within the Netlify ecosystem, Netlify could well be the best choice.

Features

- **Longest function runtime:** 15 minutes
- **Largest function size:** 50MB compressed
- **Maximum memory allocation:** 1GB
- **Languages supported natively:** JavaScript, TypeScript, Go

- **Access from front ends:** Native support
- **Authentication integration:** Netlify Identity (powered by GoTrue API)

Pricing

Netlify Functions are priced as part of the main Netlify plans (Starter, which is free; Pro, which costs $19 per month, per member; and Business, which costs $99 per month, per member). Each plan includes a volume of invocations for free (and Business includes unlimited invocations), and then overages are charged (for example, $19 per 500,000 requests and 500 runtime hours per month). Netlify also charges on bandwidth, so that might impact functions pricing, if indirectly.

www.netlify.com/products/functions/

Vercel Functions

Vercel is a competitor to Netlify. Similarly, its functions product is primarily a wrapper around AWS Lambda. As the creator of Next.js, Vercel has functions with first-party support for running the server-side Next.js calls. Vercel's functions are similar to Netlify's, in that they enable the packaging and deployment of functions within the same repository as the front-end code that calls them. Vercel functions also can be run in a variety of places, based on whether they are larger and can be slower (as with the ones that run on AWS Lambda), or are smaller and need to be faster (for example, Edge Middleware functions used for authentication, path handling, and A/B testing).

Features

- **Longest function runtime:** 15 minutes (enterprise plan)
- **Largest function size:** 50MB compressed, 250MB uncompressed
- **Maximum memory allocation:** 3008MB (enterprise plan)
- **Languages supported natively:** Node.js, Go, Python, Ruby
- **Access from front ends:** Native support
- **Authentication integration:** Vercel integrates with a variety of authentication providers, including Auth0, Firebase Authentication, and Cognito

Pricing

Vercel includes an amount of GB-hours for its Serverless functions that run on AWS Lambda within each of its plans, and then charges extra per allotment of additional GB-hours. Additionally, Vercel's Edge Middleware functions include one million invocations per month; additional invocations can be purchased in the more expensive plans.

https://vercel.com/docs/concepts/functions

Cloudflare Workers

Cloudflare, which runs one of the biggest edge networks in the world, launched its Cloudflare Workers product in 2018 as a way of running custom code as close to clients as possible. Cloudflare workers are most similar to the AWS Lambda@Edge, Netlify Edge Functions, and Vercel Edge Middleware Functions, running small amounts of code very quickly.

Since the release of Cloudflare Workers, Cloudflare has released a number of other related Serverless products in its Developer Platform, including Workers KV, a key-value store that Workers can leverage; R2, object storage that Workers can leverage; and Pages, a platform for building and deploying front-end web applications.

Features

- **Longest function runtime:** 30 seconds for Workers, 15 minutes for Scheduled Workers
- **Largest function size:** 1MB
- **Maximum memory allocation:** 128MB
- **Languages supported natively:** JavaScript, TypeScript
- **Access from front ends:** Native support
- **Authentication integration:** None (have to custom-build it using Workers KV)

Pricing

Cloudflare Workers charge for request volume and duration. At scale, Cloudflare sells the Unbound plan, which includes one million requests per month and then charges $0.15 per million additional requests; it includes 400,000 GBps of duration per month and then charges $12.50 per million GBps.

https://developers.cloudflare.com/workers/

Appendix E

Directory: Managed Services

One of the most powerful and easiest ways to start building a Serverless application, or turning an existing application into one that is Serverless, is to use managed services that handle common application functions. Durable managed services tend to have better uptime, latency, stability, documentation, and developer experience than features that are built in bespoke custom code. This appendix walks through a variety of managed services that have large customer bases and likely address customer functionality better than most individual companies' bespoke solutions.

This appendix omits a number of extremely well-known services (including Stripe for billing, Sendgrid for email, and Twilio for telephony) because most companies generally use these already and do not tend to implement their functionalities from scratch. An online version of this directory is updated on a regular basis, available at servicespotting.com.

Algolia

Algolia is a search index service that takes relatively small documents (JSON) to load an index and returns search results extremely quickly, with excellent configurable options for many different search use cases (including full text, large product catalogs, and customer databases). Algolia was founded in 2012 and has been a favorite choice for Serverless application developers ever since. See Figure E.1 for an example of Algolia's web dashboard.

To the untrained eye, Algolia looks like a managed version of Elasticsearch, but it is far superior for Serverless applications—not to mention having a significantly better developer experience. Algolia is fully managed, not like the "managed" versions

Figure E.1 *The Algolia Dashboard*

of Elasticsearch that aren't multitenant and have many failure modes that fall on the developing company (such as running out of space or memory).

Algolia also has a significant number of fine-grained security options that enable untrusted front ends to query and retrieve only the data that a user is allowed to access. For example, Branch has indexes of all its insurance offers and policies, but it has independent agents who are allowed to access only the offers and policies that they have created. Algolia makes it easy, upon user provisioning, to create a unique token per agent that applies a filter on every query made directly to Algolia so that the agents have access to only their records. Additionally, Branch stores this token in Cognito user records so that the entire process of authenticating and querying the indexes does not involve a single request to any Branch back-end code.

Some Companies Using Algolia in Production

- Adobe
- Stripe
- Zendesk

Competitors

- **TypeSense (www.typesense.org):** TypeSense has most of the same features as Algolia, along with a number of features that it doesn't. It is also less truly Serverless, in that TypeSense Cloud (its managed-service offering) does not scale to zero and is not fully multitenant. TypeSense can be significantly cheaper than Algolia, so if Algolia seems excessively expensive for a given use, TypeSense might be worth checking out.

Pricing

At the time of publication, Algolia's primary product is offered with either the Standard feature set, which starts at $1 per month for 1,000 search requests and 1,000 records per month; or the Premium feature set, which starts at $1.50 per month for the same. In other words, pricing is based upon what features are needed, how many searches are happening, and how many records are in the indexes. At higher volumes of records and searches, the price goes down per record/search. For around ten million records in indexes and around ten million searches per month, Branch pays around $40,000 per year.

www.algolia.com/

Cloudinary

Cloudinary, founded in 2012, is a managed service that handles common image and video hosting and manipulation needs. Cloudinary can take uploads directly from untrusted clients; put them into a human (or automated) moderation queue (to censor inappropriate images); automatically resize, apply filters, apply watermarks, and make other changes; and then make them available via Cloudinary's CDN for rapid display everywhere. It's not necessary to have all the images uploaded from clients; Cloudinary can pull from object storage such as S3, or customers can load images directly via API or the Cloudinary console. See Figure E.2 for an example of the Cloudinary dashboard.

The most common practice for handling image manipulation for modern developers is to build flows around ImageMagick, an open-source library. Cloudinary is much more powerful, simpler, faster, and, of course, Serverless. Cloudinary has many add-ons that enable advanced manipulation and filters, including background removal, AI content analysis, moderation, and facial identification. Perhaps the best part of Cloudinary is that its API for using filters, manipulation, and add-ons

Figure E.2 *The Cloudinary Dashboard*

is implemented through URL patterns. To make a number of different versions of a source image, all that's needed is to append different paths onto the URL. This makes it easy for nondevelopers to set up different versions of each image.

Some Companies Using Cloudinary in Production

- Bombas
- Nintendo
- NBC

Competitors

- **ImageKit (www.imagekit.io):** ImageKit is a newer entrant but has built most of the same features of Cloudinary.
- **Imgix (https://imgix.com/):** Imgix has been around since before Cloudinary (2011), but it recently added Serverless features that match Cloudinary's (such as file upload from browser).

Pricing

Cloudinary prices by use, which encompasses the number of images, transformations, images served, and users with access to the Cloudinary console. Paid accounts start at $89 per month, which includes 225 credits and access for 3 users. Each credit can be used for 1,000 transformations, 1GB storage, or 1GB network transfer.

www.cloudinary.com/

Segment

Segment was founded in 2011, at a time when services such as Google Analytics and Mixpanel were increasingly popular, easy ways for companies to better understand the users on their web applications. These services worked by including JavaScript snippets into application code. For some uses, the application called service-specific functions to tell the service about something happening within the application (for example, identifying the user or tracking an action).

Segment was built to sit in front of all these services and be the central collector and distributor of identification and event information to all the downstream services that could use that information. When Segment gained popularity, more services sprang up that leveraged this centralized flow of user events (some are mentioned later in this appendix). See Figure E.3 for an example of how this is depicted in the Segment dashboard.

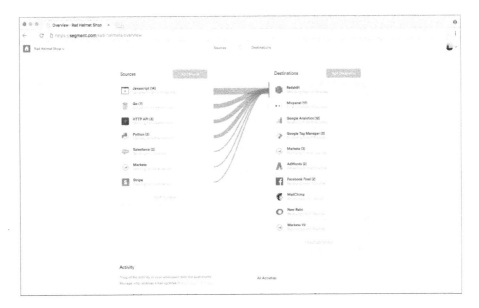

Figure E.3 *The Segment Dashboard*

At its core, Segment is an event bus that captures individual user events, transmits those to other services so that every service has the same set of information and events in real time, and saves the full event history to a data warehouse. Segment has a fantastic uptime and low latency history, and it has been the standard-bearer for the problem it solves since it created the category.

Because of the price, many architects do not start with Segment in greenfield application architecture. However, for any application that needs to grow quickly with many stakeholders across the business (such as performance marketing, customer experience, and revenue operations), it is almost certainly cheaper to build with Segment from the beginning, based on the cost of stakeholder time in managing bespoke user data information.

Some Companies Using Segment in Production

- ABInBev
- FOX
- Levi's

Competitors

- **Freshpaint (www.freshpaint.io/):** Freshpaint is a Segment competitor that is focused on not needing developer time and effort to identify the events to track (a feature that Segment also advertises but is less full featured than Freshpaint's).
- **RudderStack (www.rudderstack.com/):** RudderStack is younger and quite similar to Segment in terms of core features.
- **mParticle (www.mparticle.com/):** mParticle, founded in 2013, started as event tracking for mobile apps and has since expanded to the web.

Pricing

Segment prices by monthly tracked user (MTU). For each of these users, many Segment plans restrict the number of API calls that can be made per MTU (in aggregate)—for example, 250 is a common limit for the number of API calls per month, per MTU. As of publication, Segment's paid accounts started at $120 per month for 10,000 MTUs and an additional $10 per month, per each additional 1,000 MTUs.

www.segment.com/

Customer.io

Customer.io, founded in 2012, provides a way to use identity and event stream data from a service such as Segment.com to trigger communications campaigns, usually through email, text messaging, and in-app notifications (see Figure E.4). These campaigns can run for weeks through branching logic and dynamic text. They can be targeted at achieving a goal (for example, to have someone purchase something), at which point they end. Customer.io can also trigger other types of activities than direct communications, such as making webhook calls or sending messages to slack.

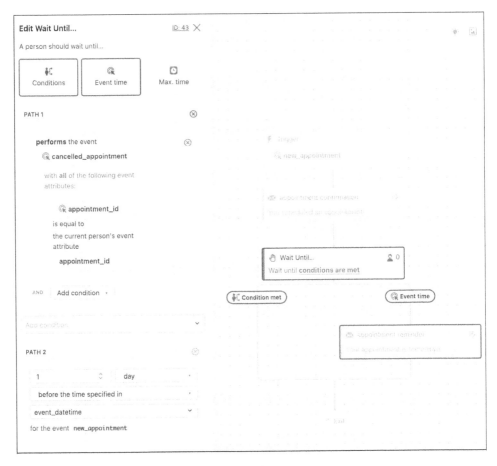

Figure E.4 *Example Customer.io Workflow*

Some Companies Using Customer.io in Production

- Notion
- Pillpack
- Mapbox

Competitors

- **Braze (www.braze.com/):** Braze started as a mobile-app communications service and has expanded into web applications, email, and SMS. Braze has a marquee client list (including Draft Kings, GrubHub, and HBO) and provides more robust client onboarding than Customer.io.

- **Iterable (www.iterable.com):** Iterable, founded in 2013, initially targeted marketing departments and built a variety of widgets that could be leveraged within applications, similar to a message center. It has a very similar feature set today as Customer.io.

Pricing

Customer.io prices per active profile, which is different from many similar services that price per monthly active user. This means that Customer.io charges for profiles that are not getting any communications, although it is possible to remove profiles, if desired. The Customer.io entry-level plan is $150 per month, which includes up to 8,000 profiles; beyond that, pricing is handled by enterprise sales staff.

https://customer.io/

Lob

Lob, founded in 2013, provides an API-to-physical-mail gateway (see Figure E.5). Using the Lob API, Branch sends personalized marketing postcards, insurance policy information, and refund checks out of the Branch bank accounts. The Lob API allows arbitrary content to be sent (for example, an on-demand created PDF or a Lob template that has been dynamically filled out) to an arbitrary address, with a variety of controls that enable manual or automated review before papers are printed and the letters are mailed. Lob also integrates with bank accounts to enable physical checks to be sent in the mail, alongside other printed content. Branch uses Segment events to trigger Lob to send out customized mail to potential customers, printing a custom QR code and details of their insurance offer directly on a postcard.

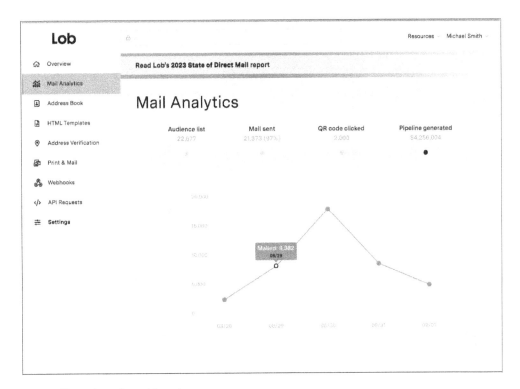

Figure E.5 *The Lob Dashboard*

Some Companies Using Lob in Production

- Clover
- Marley Spoon
- Booking.com

Competitors

- **Postal.io (https://postal.io/):** Postal, a newer entrant, does not support sending checks, but it does help automate sending corporate gifts and postal mail.

Pricing

Lob charges a monthly subscription fee; as the fee increases, it allows access to an increased feature set (more users, more mailings, better analytics, and increased security features). It also offers a price per each page or mailing, which decreases with increases in commitments. At the time of publication, the most affordable plan was $260 per month; mailing prices started at $0.51 per postcard and $0.77 per letter.

www.lob.com

Smarty

Smarty is a managed service based on address resolution and correction (see Figure E.6). Many companies use Google Maps APIs for address autocompletion and identifying information about specific addresses (such as geolocation details). However, Smarty's options could be better. Google has fairly restrictive licensing, and its location database is built around point-of-interest information; Smarty's, on the other hand, is built on government data, such as the U.S. Postal Service deliverability database, as well as tax assessors' location databases.

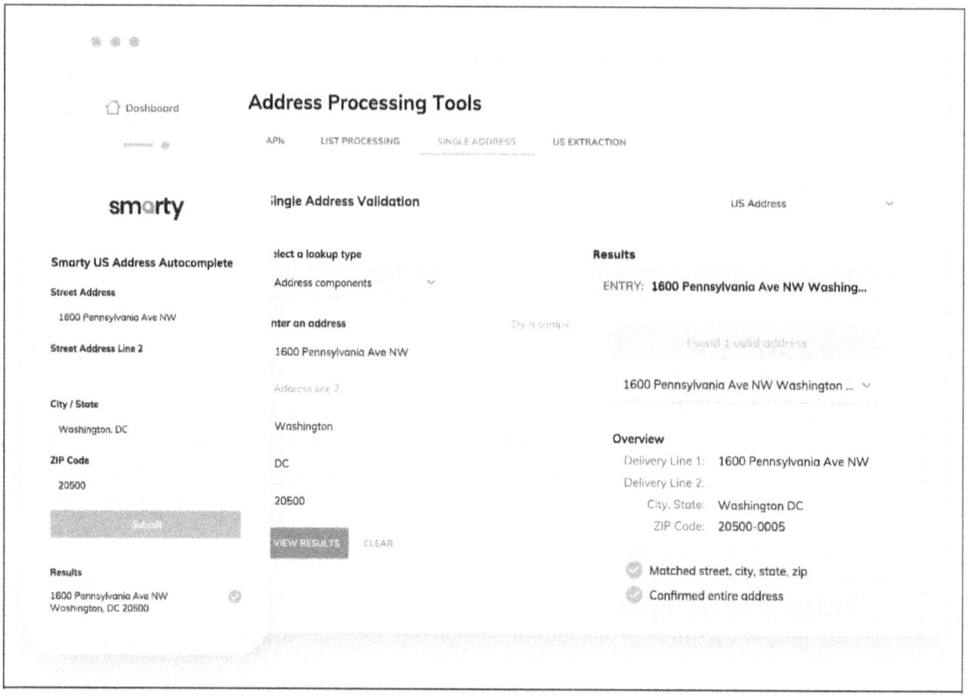

Figure E.6 *Example Smarty Address Autocomplete*

Smarty is therefore better at identifying addresses for the purpose of direct mail, as well as for matching to property databases. Additionally, Smarty is more customizable and has less restrictive licensing terms. At scale, Smarty is also significantly less expensive.

Some Companies Using Smarty in Production

- AT&T
- Microsoft
- Netflix

Competitors

- **Google Place Autocomplete (https://developers.google.com/maps/documentation/javascript/place-autocomplete):** Google Places and Maps have similar capabilities to Smarty, but they are more expensive, are more restrictive in licensing, and, for many uses, have a less accurate underlying address database.

Pricing

At lower request volumes, Smarty tends to price around $0.01 per lookup, with unlimited plans available for purchase at higher volumes.

www.smarty.com/

DocRaptor

The DocRaptor API generates PDFs from HTML and CSS on demand (see Figure E.7). DocRaptor uses an excellent underlying commercial technology called Prince, which has been rendering HTML to PDF for more than a decade (but it must be run locally if it is licensed directly). Prince has a number of unique extensions to CSS, so it's possible to build out a web page with specific details in the primary CSS that tell Prince exactly how to handle page breaks and margins, among other typesetting configurations.

DocRaptor orchestrates Prince through a simple API, taking the HTML (and CSS) as input and returning a binary PDF, or hosting the PDF for a specifiable amount of time and returning the URL. DocRaptor is an excellent choice for any

Figure E.7 *DocRaptor Marketing Page*

company that needs to provide PDFs (such as invoices or dynamic output of content, without relying on the browser to correctly format for print).

Some Companies Using DocRaptor in Production

- Accenture
- Shopify
- Square

Competitors

- **PDFMonkey (www.pdfmonkey.io/):** PDFMonkey isn't completely feature compatible with DocRaptor because it relies on rendering in Chrome to generate a PDF.

Pricing

DocRaptor charges per document, starting at $0.12 per PDF with a commitment of $15 per month, and going up to $0.025 cents per PDF with a commitment of $1,000 per month. A higher level includes unlimited PDF generation. DocRaptor also charges separately for PDF hosting, if that feature is desired.

www.docraptor.com/

Prismic

Prismic is a headless CMS, meaning that it provides a web-based interface that enables designers to create content templates, allows creators to make specific content (such as blog entries, primary website content, and help text), and permits developers to integrate via API to display the information within bespoke web applications (see Figure E.8). It also allows nontechnical stakeholders to create and update content themselves, without needing technical resources, while still making sure that all content looks and feels like every part of custom-built applications.

Figure E.8 *Example Prismic.io Workflow Management*

Some Companies Using Prismic in Production

- Digital Ocean
- Klarna
- New York Times

Competitors

- **Contentful (www.contentful.com/):** Contentful is sometimes viewed as a more "enterprise" option for a headless CMS.
- **Sanity (www.sanity.io/):** Sanity is another well-respected choice as a headless CMS, recently chosen as the best option by G2.

Pricing

Prismic prices primarily based on the number of users who need access to create templates and content, and secondarily based on enterprise-level features such as backups and SSO. The base Prismic corporate plan starts at $100 per month and includes access for up to 25 users.

www.prismic.io/

Flatfile

Flatfile, founded in 2018, solves the common problem of needing to import formatted files (for example, from Excel) into an application. There are so many different file types and formats that all contain essentially the same information, and no company has deep expertise in handling all the various edge cases. Flatfile enables companies to build a branded experience that takes common file types, helps end users map to the expected fields, and delivers the resulting data, formatted cleanly, in a variety of ways to the application (see Figure E.9).

Some Companies Using Flatfile in Production

- ClickUp
- ParrotMob

Figure E.9 *Example Flatfile Workflow*

Competitors

- **CSVBox (https://csvbox.io/):** CSVBox targets a smaller/midsize business market and allows self-signup (Flatfile is enterprise sales only, as of the time of publication).

  https://flatfile.com/

QuotaGuard

Serverless back-end architectures are multitenant, and cloud providers automatically fail over for the application. This has one downside that can impact the capability to implement some services: no consistent set of IP addresses from which requests will originate. Branch uses several data providers that require knowing source IPs as an element of authentication. QuotaGuard operates an HTTPS proxy, allowing back-end code to make requests through a known set of IP addresses (see Figure E.10).

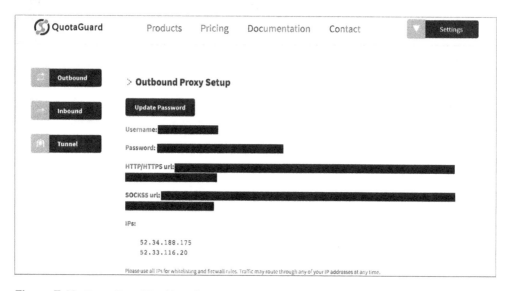

Figure E.10 *QuotaGuard Dashboard*

Production Use and Competitors

QuotaGuard has been around for several years at the time of publication, but it has been more of a niche product and doesn't have any published marquee clients (other than Branch!). QuotaGuard has been a consistently performant and reliable service for Branch.

The primary competitor for QuotaGuard is to proxy requests through dedicated virtual network infrastructure within a cloud (for example, a VPC within AWS).

Pricing

QuotaGuard pricing is based on the number of requests handled per month. For $29 per month, QuotaGuard will handle 20,000 requests. For $259 per month, it will handle a million requests.

www.quotaguard.com/

Basis Theory

Basis Theory is a tokenization service that allows any company to tokenize any information (such as credit cards and Social Security numbers) directly from client applications. That information then can be used without putting a significant compliance burden on the company. Basis Theory entirely handles the compliance burden of handling sensitive information: It receives the information directly from the client and performs all transmission through a variety of different methods (including pass-through proxy posting and using "Reactors" built for specific services, such as Stripe, as seen in Figure E.11) without the information ever touching company-controlled servers, virtual machines, or containers.

Basis Theory has a variety of interface options, but it most commonly works like Stripe Elements, a custom-styled set of embedded components within applications that send information directly to Basis Theory's servers. Basis Theory handles being PCI compliant (among other standards) and providing access to the tokenization information.

Production Use and Competitors

Basis Theory is a fairly new company, as of the time of publication. Branch uses Basis Theory in production and has found it to be performant and reliable, but Basis Theory does not presently have any other published customer case studies.

Figure E.11 *Basis Theory Workflow Example*

Basis Theory has two competitors, VGS (www.verygoodsecurity.com/) and Sky-flow (www.skyflow.com). However, neither has a completely Serverless architecture that is designed to work seamlessly with front ends directly. Additionally, neither competitor has self-signup capabilities (enterprise sales only).

Pricing

Basis Theory prices per monthly active token: Any time a token is written or read in a month, it qualifies as active. If a token is dormant (only stored) during a month, it is not billed. Pricing starts at $0.10 per monthly active token.

www.basistheory.com/

Upstash

Many useful open-source applications are designed to be run on individual containers or virtual machines and do not have truly Serverless offerings. Upstash is working to solve that problem, starting with Redis and Kafka (see Figure E.12). Upstash uses Cloudflare Workers and Fastly's Compute@Edge, in combination with a global database, to provide extremely low-latency, infinitely scalable, multitenant versions of these helpful applications.

Figure E.12 *Upstash Feature Grid*

Production Use and Competitors

Upstash is a fairly new company, as of the time of publication. Branch uses Upstash in production and has found it to be performant and reliable, but Upstash does not presently have other published customer case studies.

Upstash competition is using the open-source services that Upstash runs, but via managed hosting, but that would not be Serverless.

Pricing

Upstash charges per use, with an entry-level plan for Redis starting at $0.20 per 100,000 commands.

www.upstash.com/

Index

T

Printed in August 2024
by Rotomail Italia S.p.A., Vignate (MI) - Italy